P9-DSV-226

FOUR PLAYS BY SOPHOCLES

FOUR PLAYS BY SOPHOCLES

NEWLY TRANSLATED BY THEODORE HOWARD BANKS

Ajax

The Women of Trachis

Electra

Philoctetes

NEW YORK · OXFORD UNIVERSITY PRESS · 1966

Copyright © Oxford University Press, Inc., 1966

Electra, copyright © Theodore Howard Banks, 1960
Ajax, copyright © Theodore Howard Banks, 1961

Library of Congress Catalogue Card Number: 66-15419

No performance or reading of these translations
may be given unless a license has been obtained
in advance from the publisher, acting as the
author's representative, and no copy of these
translations or any part thereof may be re-
produced for any purpose whatsoever by any
printing or duplicating or photographic or other
method without written permission obtained in
advance from the publisher.

PRINTED IN THE UNITED STATES OF AMERICA

TO

Carol, Janet, and Bill

CONTENTS

INTRODUCTION

GREEK DRAMA

GREEK civilization reached its peak in the Athens of the fifth century B.C., expressing itself in political organization, science, history, philosophy, and the arts; music, painting, sculpture, architecture, poetry, and drama. Some of the accomplishments of this period, tragedy for one, have never been surpassed. Yet since civilization is more than art, Greek tragedy cannot be fully understood without reference to other aspects of Athenian life.

Principally because the country was broken up by mountains, the Greeks never achieved national unity but remained divided into a large number of city-states, which were grouped into two systems of alliances headed by Athens and Sparta. These states consisted of a walled city that dominated a small, usually self-contained, country district. Attica, the district controlled by Athens, was exceptionally big, yet it was smaller than Rhode Island. Minor skirmishes and shifts of allegiance kept the political situation unstable until the outbreak of the Peloponnesian War. Continuing from 460 B.C. to 404 B.C., this clash finally ended in the destruction of the Athenian empire by Sparta. Although resting on a basis of slavery, these city-states, particularly Athens, attained a considerable degree of democracy. Many questions were decided directly by the vote of the whole body of the citizens, important political and religious offices were held in rotation, and a sense of belonging to a community was highly developed. Many things that we now think of as personal were then communal, and one of the most important of these was drama.

Plays were performed annually during the spring festival in honor of Dionysus, the god of wine and of the general fertility of nature. A large part of this festival was devoted to three poetical contests, presented in the theater of Dionysus. Seating seventeen thousand people, this was situated in a locality sacred to the god. An altar stood in the center of the orchestra, and the priest of Dionysus witnessed the performances from a seat in the front row. The three contests were in the dithyramb, an ode in honor of Dionysus, sung and danced by a chorus of fifty; in comedy; and in tragedy. On the last three days of the festival, three poets submitted four plays: three tragedies, either a trilogy or on independent themes, and a semi-comic piece called a satyr play. These plays were carefully rehearsed and elaborately produced, and were judged by a selected panel of citizens. To be chosen as one of the competing poets was in itself an honor; and to win first prize was a very high honor. The plays dealt with serious moral issues, illustrated by episodes in the lives of mythical heroes like Prometheus, or semi-historical members of ancient royal houses such as those of Athens, Thebes, or Mycenae. The main outlines of the stories were traditional and therefore familiar to the audience, but the poets were at liberty to modify or invent details. Given the circumstances of performance, the mood of the spectators must in general have been serious, although there were occasions on which they shouted down a play which did not come up to their expectations. Greek tragedy, then, was essentially civic and religious.

It was, however, far more than a succession of moral lessons. It was a highly developed art, though its form was severely limited and its conventions rigid. The plays were given, as we have seen, in the open air, in a huge theater. Necessarily, the actors would appear tiny, their expressions could not be seen, and their voices could hardly carry. Therefore, they wore shoes a foot high and masks in which were inserted small speaking trumpets. Presumably the acting was highly stylized, since the characters were almost symbolic, a quality emphasized by the masks. These characters were limited to eight or ten, exclusive of the chorus, and up to the time of Sophocles no more than two could appear or at any rate speak in any one scene. Indeed, the introduction of the third actor was one of Sophocles' chief contributions, since by this means he greatly increased the range of possible dramatic effects. The difference may be made clear by comparing his early *Antigone*, whose scenes are almost all dialogues, with the scenes in his late *Oedipus at Colonus* between Oedipus, Theseus, and Antigone, or between Oedipus, Polyneices, and Antigone. Yet the number of relationships that can be established between even three actors is still extremely limited. The plots were concerned with a single main episode in the life of the hero — for example, Oedipus' discovery of his identity — and the action usually, but not necessarily, took place in one day and in one place. Even with these conventions Greek drama is similar in its essentials to modern drama.

It is the chorus that marks off Greek drama as a distinct form of art. Just as modern drama originated in the singing in the medieval church services, so Greek drama originated in the singing of the dithyramb, which, as we have seen, was a religious ode. Gradually stanzas sung by separate sections of the chorus evolved into spoken dialogue, but even in the case of Aeschylus, Sophocles' immediate predecessor, the chorus, still numbering fifty, is so prominent that his plays are more like modern oratorios than dramas. Sophocles cut the chorus to fifteen and reduced its importance in the plot, but with him it remains an integral part of the play, since it consists of a group of people whose presence is dramatically appropriate. Thought of as a unit, it often speaks through the mouth of the chorus leader, or choragus. Occasionally it influences the action of the play through its advice, expostulation, and so forth, but its chief function is to react emotionally to the action taking place before it. It philosophizes, expresses joy at the anticipated triumph of the hero or sorrow at his misfortune, prays to the gods, and the like. It expresses these emotions by singing or intoning intricate lyric poems to an accompaniment of music and dance steps. Except for a fragment of a Euripides chorus none of the music and no description of the dance patterns have survived, but we may reasonably assume that both music and dance had reached an artistic level comparable to the text. The suggestion has been made, for example, that Sophocles fixed the chorus at fifteen to allow a variety of unbalanced groupings. Obviously, such a combination of poetry, singing, music, and dancing must have had a powerful aesthetic effect. Even when the plays are merely read, the chorus serves not only to divide them into a series of contrasting and climactic scenes but also to introduce a great range of mood, triumphant, bitter, apprehensive, plaintive, etc. The effects are entirely different from those produced by the occasional songs in a Shakespearean play, since each Sophoclean ode occurs at a definite break in the action and serves as dramatic heightening as well as dramatic relief. It should be emphasized that the chorus is not the mouthpiece of Sophocles, expressing his personal feelings, but a dramatic entity, expressing emotions natural under the circumstances in which it finds itself. Everything considered, the closest modern equivalent to a tragedy of Sophocles is not a play but a grand opera.

THE LIFE OF SOPHOCLES (*c.* 496–406 B.C.)

Although Sophocles lived to the extreme age of ninety, and although he was a prominent figure in the life of his time, we know very little about him. He was noted for his youthful beauty and his skill in dancing and music. He led, with his lyre, the paean celebrating the naval victory over the Persians at Salamis. He took part, as was customary, in the acting of his plays but was forced to stop because of his weak voice. As a citizen he held the usual offices, being General at least twice. He was associated in some way with the cult of Asclepius, the god of healing. These facts, together with some rather trivial anecdotes, are all that we know about his private life.

His artistic career was extraordinarily prolific and successful, although only seven of one hundred and twenty-odd plays have survived. In the annual competition during the festival of Dionysus, he won first place twenty times (and we must remember that each victory involved four of his plays), and was never worse than second.

THE PLAYS

There is a fair consensus about the dates of composition of the four plays in this volume as follows:

> *Ajax c.* 440
> *The Women of Trachis* the 430's or 420's
> *Electra c.* 420
> *Philoctetes c.* 409

As to their evaluation, even if the critics were far more nearly in agreement than they are, it would be impossible here to give a full analysis. All that can be done is to offer in each case an interpretation of the central problem that seems correct.

About the character of Ajax himself there is little disagreement. He is a powerful figure, towering over the others, but limited and essentially selfish. His ambition, noble in itself, to be a great warrior is so overwhelming that he disdains the help of the gods in attaining it. He is shamed by the award of Achilles' armor to Odysseus and by Athena's driving him to kill in a fit of madness cattle instead of Agamemnon and Menelaus. He does not feel that he has ever been wrong, but simply that he has been treated unjustly by the kings and by the goddess. His honor is gone. Hence he has no alternative but suicide. This will be a noble death, the only way by which he can prove to his father that he is not a coward. But his suicide occurs about half-way through the action, and what follows seems at first sight to be anti-climax. Many critics feel that the play lacks unity, one of them going so far as to say that Sophocles ran out of material and had to start over. The play, however, is unified. This is due partly to the fact that Ajax is the dominant figure to the end. His suicide will not be noble, his pre-eminence will not be acknowledged, unless his funeral rites are properly conducted. Chiefly, however, it is due to the fact that the character of Ajax is contrasted to that of Odysseus, who begins and ends the action. At the beginning of the opening scene Odysseus is afraid of Ajax; at its end he pities him because Ajax, like all men, is helpless before the power of the gods. In the closing scene of the play he insists that Ajax be given the customary burial because he himself will someday need burial. The time for hatred has passed. All humanity shares a common fate. Odysseus is not generous, merely clear-sighted. He is calm, sensible, impartial, and far more admirable than the small-minded and spiteful Agamemnon and Menelaus. He has, however, no spark of greatness or heroism. The play, therefore, balances one ideal of life against another.

Similarly *The Women of Trachis* has been thought to lack unity. If Deianeira is the central figure, then the section devoted to Heracles is merely tacked on. If Heracles is the central figure, he appears far too late. The play, however, like *Ajax*, is unified through the balancing of one character against another. The first three-quarters of the action is devoted to Deianeira. She is charmingly feminine, without any of the hardness of Electra or Antigone. She is deeply and unselfishly in love, although too human to bear the thought of sharing her husband with another woman under the same roof. She pities her rival, Iole. She is timid and indecisive, hesitating to act even in self-defense. When she learns that she has killed her husband, she has no interest in explaining the purity of her intentions and in clearing her name. Her suicide leaves her more pathetic than heroic. Against her is set the violent, self-centered, ruthlessly efficient, intensely masculine figure of Heracles. He is not presented, as he generally is elsewhere, as the heroic benefactor of mankind, but as a callous husband, indifferent to the guilt or innocence of his wife, as well as a callous father, insisting on his son's marriage to Iole. He is constantly referred to in the earlier part of the play and nearly always in terms of violence. He enters bewailing his physical wreckage. The frail Deianeira is overwhelmed when she tries to cope with such a man, and it is significant that, son of Zeus though he is, Heracles is always merely a man. Sophocles omits his apotheosis. He is going to his funeral pyre simply to be burned to death, not to be given immortality on Olympus. But her frailty destroys his strength. Neither Deianeira nor Heracles is the protagonist. It is notable that the titular role is assigned to the Chorus. Heracles has obvious moral flaws, but they are not the direct cause of his death. Furthermore, Deianeira speaks of his physical passion as something beyond his control, as a disease, an infliction of the gods, rather than as a weakness of character. Nor has he deserved the fearful suffering he has to endure before his death. Still less does Deianeira deserve her fate. The play ends in a burst of bitterness. Hyllus denounces the cruelty of the gods, who are shamed by what has happened. The Chorus say that everything that has been seen, however dreadful, is Zeus.

In *Electra* the controversy has centered on the closing lines. Orestes has killed Clytemnestra and has just driven Aegisthus into the palace to kill him there. The Chorus then end the play by saying that though the house of Atreus has seen struggle and suffering

> With this day's enterprise you have found freedom
> And are made whole at last.

In view of the fact that the highly popular trilogy of Aeschylus, *The Oresteia*, produced some forty years earlier, dealt with the fearful retribution that at once came upon Orestes, this is an astonishing statement. Is Sophocles condoning matricide? Too much can be made of the Chorus's concluding verses. In nearly all the plays they are merely pious tags, and represent the Chorus's point of view, not the playwright's. In the course of the action of this play, the Chorus have become completely sympathetic with Electra and feel that the murders are entirely justified. It should be remembered that even in *The Oresteia* Electra is not punished in any way. The stigma attaches only to the actual killer. In any case, the moral issue, if not irrelevant, is strictly subordinate. Orestes is a minor figure, the *deus ex machina*. He begins the play by planning the revenge and ends the play by executing it, but this action is merely a frame for Electra. Furthermore Orestes is hardly characterized. He is almost surgical in his approach to his task, and seems really moved only in the recognition scene when he realizes for the first time the extent of Electra's suffering. His reaction to Electra is important, not his reaction to anything else. The bulk of the play is a detailed study of Electra's character: her unshaken loyalty to her father, her contempt for her sister, her fierce hatred and defiance of her mother and Aegisthus, her courage in not yielding to persecution, her momentary despair, her resolution to kill Aegisthus herself, her savage triumph at the end. The only thing that qualifies this harsh impression is her love for Orestes. He is not merely her instrument of vengeance but the child she tenderly remembers nursing. Moreover, she is given ample excuse for her hatred. Her father is made virtually innocent in his sacrifice of Iphigenia, the act that led to his own death. Her mother and Aegisthus are blackened in every possible way. She wins, if not like Deianeira our love, certainly our admiration.

Though *Philoctetes* lacks any character of the heroic proportions of *Ajax* or *Electra* and though its theme is less sensational than vengeance or suicide, it is, nevertheless, a play of great interest. It contains a complicated plot resolved by the spectacular intervention of the divine Heracles. Its interaction of character is unique in Greek drama. Neoptolemus, persuaded at the outset by Odysseus to act against the dictates of his conscience in the interest of expediency, gradually shifts to the side of Philoctetes, partly through sympathy for his prolonged suffering, partly through admiration for his point of view, which he realizes he himself shares. Philoctetes, in turn, is softened by the warmth and nobility of Neoptolemus. He abandons his refusal to return to human society and declares his readiness to defend Neoptolemus, if necessary, when they have returned home. At this point the critics part company. Some maintain that the play is merely an interesting stage spectacle, and that no larger issues are involved. For them Heracles presents no problem. He is simply the *deus ex machina* that brings the action to the conclusion prescribed by the myth. For others, and for me, this position is unsatisfactory. Larger issues are always involved in Sophocles' works. Here the characters are to some extent symbols. Odysseus, in his attempt to force Philoctetes to return to Troy and save the Greeks, represents the demands of the social order. Philoctetes, in his resentment of the cruel treatment he has received and his fear of additional future suffering, represents the freedom of the individual to lead his own life. Philoctetes wins his struggle. Odysseus gives up, and Neoptolemus agrees to take him home. Yet, when they arrive they will be inactive; they will take no part in the Trojan War. At this moment Heracles appears. In addition to being a god, he may well be also the personification of a new and nobler ideal that dawns upon Philoctetes. Neoptolemus has sacrificed his future for him. Self-sacrifice is nobler than self-service, friendship nobler than isolation. The will of Zeus, as he is told and as he has come to see for himself, is that he and Neoptolemus together, as comrades in arms, whatever suffering may be in store, will serve the state and in so doing will win victory, glory, the happiness of a heroic life.

THE TRANSLATION

Since translation is an art, the translator must try to satisfy himself primarily, and the particular form he chooses for his attempt cannot be logically defended. It can only be described. The form of these translations is as follows: most of the dialogue is in blank verse, and special care was taken to catch the idioms and cadences of spoken, rather than written, language. Some dialogue, in the passages where there is a change of meter in the original, is in heroic couplet, heroic quatrains, or irregular rhymed stanzas.

The choruses and a number of lyric passages in the dialogue are in rhymed stanzas. These stanzas are in pairs and thus preserve a distinctive feature of the Greek. The first stanza, the strophe, sets the rhythmic pattern, and the second stanza, the antistrophe, repeats it exactly. The pattern of stanzas three and four is likewise identical but differs from the first pattern. Occasionally a chorus has an odd stanza, an epode, with an individual pattern. There is, then, repetition within each chorus, but the rhyme scheme and rhythms of one chorus are never repeated in any other. Each chorus is a lyric poem which differs in mood, and therefore in form, from all the rest.

The choruses are distinguished from the dialogue in two other ways. Because they are lyric poems, in which people are not so much speaking as singing, their vocabulary is somewhat fuller and more elaborate. Also, in them, the translation is of necessity less close, since the thought must be paraphrased or expanded to provide rhymes. Rhymed stanzas contrast sharply with the dialogue, however, and this contrast provides an aesthetic effect comparable to that of the Greek. Furthermore, experience with this text has shown that when the plays are produced, the choruses lend themselves readily to group speaking, to musical accompaniment, and to dance interpretation. The resulting aesthetic effect is markedly unlike that produced by a modern play. To sum up, therefore, it may be well to repeat what was said earlier. Even with all the suspense, the clash of personalities, and the climactic emotion of Greek drama, the contemporary art form that most closely resembles it is grand opera.

Ajax

CHARACTERS IN THE PLAY

ATHENA

AJAX

TECMESSA, *slave-concubine of* AJAX

TEUCER, *half-brother of* AJAX

ODYSSEUS

MENELAUS, *King of Sparta, husband of* HELEN

AGAMEMNON, *King of Mycenae, Commander-in-chief*

MESSENGER

CHORUS *of sailors, followers of* AJAX

AJAX

SCENE: *The Greek camp at Troy. Before the tent of* AJAX

Enter ATHENA *and* ODYSSEUS

ATHENA:
    Odysseus, I have watched you always hunting
    Your enemies down, eager to find some way
    Of seizing them. Now, where the tent of Ajax
    Here on the flank stands guard beside the ships
    I see you in pursuit of him, inspecting
    His new-made tracks in order to find out
    If he is here or not. And with your scent
    As keen as a Laconian hound's you will
    Soon trace him down, for he has just gone in
    With his face bathed in sweat and with his hands   10
    Red from a murderous sword. You do not need
    To peer inside. But come now. Let me know
    The reason for this diligent search of yours
    That with my knowledge I may give you light.

ODYSSEUS:
    Athena's voice! O dearest of the gods,
    I cannot see you but your words sound clearly,
    And my heart thrills to hear them as it thrills
    To hear a brazen trumpet cry aloud.
    You have seen me hunting everywhere for Ajax,
    My enemy who bears the mighty shield.   20
    He is the man I have followed for so long.
    Last night he did us unbelievable harm,
    If it was he — nothing is known for certain;
    We are still in the dark — and I assumed the task
    Of looking for him. All our captured herds
    Have just been found dead, and the herdsmen with them.
    Someone has slaughtered them. We all believe
    Ajax is guilty, for a man on lookout
    Who saw him bounding off across the plain,
    Alone, waving a sword smeared with fresh blood,   30
    Came to me with the news. I lost no time
    In following the scent, and I am sure
    Some tracks are his, but others puzzle me.
    I cannot think who made them. You have come
    When I most needed you. Your hand has led me
    In days gone by, and it will lead me still.

ATHENA:
> I know, Odysseus. I at once took up
> My station here to help you in your hunt.

ODYSSEUS:
> Dear mistress! Then my effort is not wasted?

ATHENA:
> No. Ajax did these things you may be sure.   40

ODYSSEUS:
> What was the reason for his senseless violence?

ATHENA:
> Achilles' armor goaded him to fury.

ODYSSEUS:
> Then why did he attack the animals?

ATHENA:
> It was your blood he thought his hand was stained with.

ODYSSEUS:
> What! Did he mean to fall upon the Greeks?

ATHENA:
> Had I been off my guard, he would have done so.

ODYSSEUS:
> What could have made him so completely reckless?

ATHENA:
> He stole upon you in the night, alone.

ODYSSEUS:
> Did he get near us? Did he reach his goal?

ATHENA:
> He reached the tent doors of your two commanders.   50

ODYSSEUS:
> What kept his eager hand from killing them?

ATHENA:
> I was the one who balked his deadly triumph,
> Darkening his eyes with tyrannous delusions,
> Turning his rage against the mingled droves
> Of sheep and oxen that the herdsmen guarded,
> Your undivided booty. Then he killed
> The horned beasts, hacking out a circle round him.
> One time he thought that those he seized and slew
> Were the two sons of Atreus; other times
> He struck down other leaders. As he raved,   60
> I spurred him back and forth, heightening his madness,
> Entangling him in fearful toils. At last
> He called a halt. Then roping all the sheep
> And oxen that were still alive, he drove them
> Inside his tent, as if his catch had been
> Men and not beasts. There he has tied them up
> And is tormenting them. But I will show
> The sight to you too, let you see his madness,

And then you can proclaim it to the Greeks.
Keep up your courage. Just to look at him   70
Will do no harm, for I will turn his eyes
Away from you. He will not see your face.
You there, binding your prisoners' arms! Come here.
Ajax, come outside. I am calling you.

ODYSSEUS:
   No, no, Athena! Do not make him come.

ATHENA:
   Quiet! Do not let yourself be called a coward.

ODYSSEUS:
   By all the gods, let him stay there inside.

ATHENA:
   Why? Up to now he has been just a man.

ODYSSEUS:
   He was my enemy, and he still is.

ATHENA:
   Is it not sweet to mock your enemy?   80

ODYSSEUS:
   To have him stay inside will be enough.

ATHENA:
   You shrink from an encounter with a madman?

ODYSSEUS:
   Yes. But I would not shrink if he were sane.

ATHENA:
   You need not, even now. He will not see you.

ODYSSEUS:
   Why not? His eyesight is the same as ever.

ATHENA:
   But I will darken it, keen as it is.

ODYSSEUS:
   Well, a god's power is limitless, I know.

ATHENA:
   Then do not speak, or move from where you are.

ODYSSEUS:
   I have no choice, much as I want to leave.

ATHENA:
   Ajax! Ajax! I am calling a second time!   90
   Is this the deference you show your helper?

                    Enter AJAX *with a blood-stained whip*

AJAX:
   Welcome Athena! Welcome, daughter of Zeus,
   My faithful ally! I will honor you
   With golden gifts to thank you for my prey.

ATHENA:
   That is well said. But tell me: is your sword
   Thoroughly soaked in the Greek army's blood?

5

AJAX:
> I do not deny it. I am proud of it.

ATHENA:
> And the sons of Atreus. Did you strike them too?

AJAX:
> Never again will they dishonor Ajax.

ATHENA:
> Then they are dead, if I have understood you.   100

AJAX:
> Dead. Let them rob me of my armor now!

ATHENA:
> So much for them. And now, Laertes' son:
> What has become of him? Did he escape?

AJAX:
> That treacherous fox! You ask me where he is?

ATHENA:
> I do. I mean Odysseus, your opponent.

AJAX:
> He is inside, my favorite prisoner.
> I am not ready yet to have him die.

ATHENA:
> What will you do first? Have you more to gain?

AJAX:
> First I will bind him to the tent pole here —

ATHENA:
> Poor man! What else will you inflict on him?   110

AJAX:
> And have his back lashed red before he dies.

ATHENA:
> Oh Ajax! Do not torture the poor wretch.

AJAX:
> In everything else have your own way, Athena.
> But that will be his punishment just the same.

ATHENA:
> Well, since his punishment will give you pleasure,
> Do what you have in mind and spare him nothing.

AJAX:
> Yes, I will go to work. But do not fail
> To stand behind me, as you did today.

> > > *Exit* AJAX

ATHENA:
> Odysseus, do you see how strong the gods are?
> Here was a man who could proceed with foresight,   120
> Who had sound judgment. Could you find his equal?

ODYSSEUS:
> No, I could not. He is my enemy,
> And yet I pity him, brought down to this,

Caught in the grip of such a grievous fate —
My fate as well as his, it seems to me,
Because I see that every living man
Is but a phantom or an empty shadow.

ATHENA:

Then after this experience, take care
Not to be boastful at the gods' expense,
Not to be arrogant because your strength   130
Is greater than another's, or your wealth.
For one day is enough to tip the scales,
And men succeed or fail. The gods love those
Who show discretion, and hate evil men.

Exeunt ATHENA *and* ODYSSEUS
Enter CHORUS OF SAILORS, *marching*

CHORUS:

Ajax, lord of the realm of Salamis
Standing firm in the sea that rings it,
    Son of Telamon, we rejoice
When all goes well with you, but when Zeus'
    Anger strikes, or the raging voice
Of slander assails you, we shrink like fluttering   140
Doves with terrified eyes, and tremble.
    Now we hear in the dawning day
Growing rumors that shame and confound us:
    Down to the meadow where horses play
You went in the darkness, swinging your flashing
Sword and slaughtering herds of cattle,
    Booty as yet unshared by the Greeks.
These are the lies Odysseus whispers
    All through the army, and when he speaks,
Many believe him, for what he says of you   150
Carries conviction. Each new hearer,
    Learning misfortune has brought you low,
Triumphs more than the man who told him,
    Openly mocking you. Every blow
Strikes home when aimed at a noble spirit;
Tales about us would be disregarded,
    For only on great men envy falls.
Yet the humble without the mighty
    Can hardly defend the city's walls.
High and low leagued together will prosper;   160
But fools can never acquire such knowledge,
    Fools like those whom we now hear rail
Loudly against you. How can we answer?
    Help us, Ajax, or we fail.
Bird-like, they flock together and chatter,
Once they know that your eye is not on them.

7

Yet in an instant, if you should come,
They would cower before the mighty vulture,
Frightened, motionless, stricken dumb.

Who drove you to fall on the beasts that belonged to
    the army?   170
  That is the clamorous tale that begot my disgrace.
Was it Artemis, daughter of Zeus, the wild bulls' goddess,
  Who was given no gift when you killed a stag in the chase,
No spoil when you triumphed in battle, and showed
    her resentment?
  Or was it the War God, angry at some slight,
Bronze-armored Ares, your support in battle,
  Who punished you with trickery in the night?

Had you been yourself, you would never have slaughtered
    the cattle,
  A deed mistaken, too wide of the mark to do.
But the gods inflict madness on men. May Zeus and
    Apollo   180
  Grant that this ugly rumor prove untrue.
And if it is untrue, if vile Odysseus
  And the great kings, in the furtive tales they spread,
Have slandered you, then leave your tent, lord Ajax,
  You lose your honor when you hide your head.
Come, rouse yourself. You have stayed away from the battle
  Too long a time, and have sat brooding there,
Letting disaster blaze up to the heavens.
  Your enemies grow bold, and everywhere
Their insolence sweeps unchecked through the breezy
    valleys.   190
  The sound of their mocking laughter is hard to bear.
    We can see no end to our sorrow.
                  Enter TECMESSA

TECMESSA:
    Sailors, men of the race of Erechtheus,
      Sprung from the soil of Athens,
    You, his crew, and all who love him
    And love the far-off house of his father
      Weep for him. Ajax, our master,
    In all his rugged strength lies prostrate
      Under a storm of affliction.
CHORUS:
    Is it anything worse than yesterday's burden?   200
      Has the darkness brought some greater woe?
    Tell us, daughter of Phrygian Teleutas.

Mighty Ajax won you in battle,
You share his bed and he loves you dearly.
    You can give us some hint, for you must know.

TECMESSA:

How can I speak? The tale is beyond words awful,
    As dreadful as death to hear of.
    Our noble Ajax is utterly ruined,
        Stricken last night with madness.
Look in the tent for proof, and you will see there   210
The victims, bathed in blood, that he has butchered,
        The sacrifice he offered.

CHORUS:

What have you told us? A tale that we cannot endure
And yet that we cannot escape. The whole of the army
    Is ringing with the news. His doom is sure
And fills me with dread. He will go to his death dishonored,
    Shamed in the eyes of all, our fiery lord,
If he slew in his frenzy herds and mounted herdsmen
        With his dark sword.

TECMESSA:

So they came from there, his captives,   220
The beasts he brought home and slaughtered.
He cut the throats of some of them. Others
He stabbed in the sides and tore to pieces.
Then he caught up two white-footed rams. The first one's
Head and tongue he cut off and flung them
    Down to the ground. Next he folded
The heavy reins of a horse's bridle
In a double thong, and flogged the other
Bound by its forelegs upright against the tent-pole.
As the lash whistled, he uttered a stream of curses   230
No mortal man but a god must have taught him.

CHORUS:

Now we should steal off quickly, furtively,
With muffled heads, or seated on the benches,
    Strain at the oars to reach the open sea.
The two kings hurl such angry threats against us
    We shall be stoned to death. We do not dare
Stay with him, subject to a fate too fearful
        For us to share.

TECMESSA:

It has run its course. The lightning no longer flashes,
The sudden violence of the storm is over.   240
His madness has died away and he is quiet,
But he still suffers. To know he is the author —
He and no other — of his own undoing
    Brings him fresh sorrow.

9

CHORUS:
> Then if his mind is clear, all may be well;
> Trouble is less important when it is past.

TECMESSA:
> Which would you choose, if you could have a choice:
> To grieve your friends while you yourself were happy,
> Or have an equal share in all their grief?

CHORUS:
> The double grief, Tecmessa, is the greater. 250

TECMESSA:
> The evil is over, then, but we are lost.

CHORUS:
> What do you mean? I do not understand.

TECMESSA:
> While he was still distracted, Ajax found
> Pleasure in his delusions, although we,
> His sane companions, suffered greatly. Now
> He has a respite, with his frenzy gone,
> And yet his sorrow masters him completely,
> While ours is no less keen. Do we not, then,
> Find two afflictions here instead of one?

CHORUS:
> Yes. And I fear some god has struck him down. 260
> Otherwise he would now be less unhappy
> Than when he still was in the throes of madness.

TECMESSA:
> And yet you may be sure those are the facts.

CHORUS:
> How did this sudden attack swoop down upon him?
> Tell us what happened. We are sufferers too.

TECMESSA:
> You shall learn everything as if you had been there.
> In the dead of night, when the torches had burned out,
> Ajax took up a two-edged sword, intent
> On creeping out upon some fruitless quest.
> Then I spoke sharply: "What are you doing, Ajax? 270
> Where are you off to? No one has called for you,
> No messenger has come, no trumpet sounded.
> Everyone in the army is asleep."
> His curt reply was the familiar saying:
> "Woman, in women silence is a virtue."
> After this lesson I said nothing. Ajax
> Went out alone. I cannot tell what happened
> While he was gone, but he brought back with him
> His booty: bulls, sheep-dogs, and woolly captives,
> All tied together. Then he attacked them fiercely, 280
> Bent up their necks and slit their throats, cut off
> Their heads, hacked them in two, and tortured them,

10

Helplessly bound, as if they had been human.
Finally he rushed headlong from the tent,
Frantically shouting to some phantom, laughing,
Taunting the sons of Atreus and Odysseus,
Boasting of how he had avenged their insults
By his attack. Then he rushed in again
And somehow, by slow stages, painfully
Came to his senses. When he saw his tent   290
Filled with the evidence that his life was ruined,
He struck at his head, gave a great cry and fell
Prostrate among the heaps of prostrate bodies
Of slaughtered sheep. He sat there on the ground,
Clutching his hair in his clenched hands, in silence,
For a long time. At last, with fearful threats,
He ordered me to tell him what had happened
And how things stood with him. Friends, I was frightened,
So that I told him everything he had done,
Everything that I knew about. At once,   300
Loud wails burst from him, cries of bitter anguish,
Different from any I had ever heard,
For he had always taught me that such weeping
Was proof of cowardice or despondency,
And when he grieved, the sound was always low,
Like the deep moaning of a bull. But now,
Utterly crushed by this calamity,
Motionless, without food or drink, he sits
Where he had fallen among the slaughtered cattle.
Clearly he has some frightful thing in mind   310
That his laments and words give hints of. Friends,
Come in and help me — that is what I came for —
Help if you can. Men in such desperate straits
May be persuaded if their friends will speak.

CHORUS:
What you have said is terrible, Tecmessa:
Ajax, our lord, driven mad by his misfortunes.

AJAX (crying out):
Oh! Oh!

TECMESSA:
Something still worse is coming. Did you hear him?
Did you hear Ajax give that piercing cry?

CHORUS:
He is still mad, or else he cannot bear   320
The sight of what his madness made him do.

AJAX:
Son! Son!

TECMESSA:
Oh! He is calling for Eurýsacés!
What can he want? Where can you be? How dreadful!

11

AJAX:

> Teucer! Where is he? Will that raid of his
> Go on forever? I am dying here.

CHORUS:

> He seems to be sane. Open the tent. To see
> Someone, if only us, perhaps will calm him.

TECMESSA:

> I will. Look there. Now you can see yourselves
> How he has acted and his own condition.   330
>
> AJAX *is revealed sitting among the dead beasts*

AJAX:

> Oh! My old friends and comrades!
> The only ones still loyal, still unshaken.
> See what a storm bursts on me, what a flood
> Swirls and surges around me,
> Great waves of blood!

CH.:

> How fearful a sight! What you have said was true.
> This is clear proof of his insanity.

AJAX:

> We embarked together, shipmates,
> My crew of veteran seamen, my strong oarsmen!
> Now in my misery I turn to you,   340
> For you alone can release me.
> Come! Kill me too.

CH.:

> Hush! Evil is not cured by further evil.
> Do not make heavier your awful fate.

AJAX:

> Here is the warrior, bold, unflinching, dauntless!
> I proved my courage — Look! — by striking dead
> The unsuspecting cattle. Oh, how shameful!
> How could I fall so low?

TEC.: Ajax, my lord! Please do not speak so! Please!

AJAX: Out of my sight! Get out! Get out of here!   350

CH.: We beg you to listen, to control yourself.

AJAX: I have brought down a curse upon my head.

> I let them go,
> Let the scoundrels slip through my fingers, and slaughtered
> The cattle and goats instead,
> Spilling the dark blood of those splendid creatures.

CH.: Why do you grieve for what is past and gone?
A deed once done can never be undone.

AJAX: There is no one so vile, so loathsome as you, Odysseus!

> Spying on everyone, spying everywhere,   360

Always an eager accomplice in any outrage.
  Now you are laughing for joy.
CH.: Laughter and grief are given us by the gods.
AJAX: If I could see him, broken though I am —
CH.: No boasting now, not in your desperate plight.
AJAX: Zeus, father of my fathers, hear my prayer!
    Let me destroy
That cunning fox, that hated villain.
  Let me destroy that pair
Of brother kings. Then let me live no longer.   370
TEC.: Pray that my life may end as well as yours.
Why should I stay alive when you are dead?

AJAX:

    Darkness, my only daylight,
  Gloom of the underworld, my only brightness,
    Take me into your dwelling!
I am unworthy, such a man as I,
To ask help from the race of the immortals,
  Or from men who live but a moment;
  For Zeus's daughter, that mighty goddess,
  Goads me, drives me to my destruction.   380
    Where can I fly?
  Where can I go to find rest?
The man that I was once has perished
With these creatures around me, the quarry
  I sought in a madman's quest.
And the army will brandish
  Their swords and cut me to pieces.
TEC.: How sad to hear such words from so splendid a man,
Words that before this he would never have uttered.

AJAX:

    Sea with your turbulent pathways,   390
Caverns and wooded pastures that border the waters,
    Too long, too long you have seen me
Lingering out my days on the Trojan shore.
But now you shall see me a living man no longer.
    This all may know for certain.
  O river Scamander, flowing beside us,
  Friend of the Greeks, you shall look upon Ajax
    No more, no more:
  A man — for I will boast —
In the eyes of Troy unequaled by any   400
Who came from the land of Hellas,
    Unequaled in all the host.
  Now you see him humbled
  Here in the dust before you.
CH.: I cannot stop you from speaking, nor can I bear
To have you speak, who have suffered such heavy grief.

13

AJAX:

What misery! Who could have thought my name
Would be the very echo of my fate?
Time and again I cry my name aloud,
Voicing my agony in its syllables.   410
My father in the land of Ida here
Won by his bravery the fairest prize
In all the army and brought honor home;
But I, his son, who have come after him
To the same country, no less strong than he
And no less great in my accomplishments,
Die in disgrace among the Greeks. And yet
This much is certain: had Achilles lived,
Had he been called upon to give his arms
To the man whose courage made him worthiest of them,   420
Then no one would have laid his hands on them
Before I did. Instead, the sons of Atreus
Devised the scheme of giving them to a scoundrel,
Brushing aside my triumphs. Never again
Would they have made a mockery of justice
Had not my eyes been dazed and my mind twisted
So that I missed my aim. But as it was,
Fierce-eyed Athena, that invincible goddess,
Struck down the hand I would have raised against them,
Sent me off reeling in a fit of madness,   430
And stained me with the blood of all these beasts.
Now those two laugh at me for having escaped
In spite of me. But if a god is cruel,
Even a wicked man eludes his betters.
What shall I do now? For beyond a doubt
I am loathed by the gods, detested by the Greeks,
Hated by Troy and the whole countryside.
Shall I desert this roadstead, leave the sons
Of Atreus, and go home across the Aegean?
And when I get there, how shall I face my father?   440
How will he bring himself to look at me,
Stripped of all honor, when he wore himself
A splendid crown of fame? I cannot do it.
Then shall I go to Troy, launch an attack
Against the walls, fight with them single-handed,
And lose my life in doing some great deed?
No, that might please the sons of Atreus.
Out of the question. Somehow I must find
A way of letting my old father know
His son is not a coward. It is shameful   450
To hope for a long life that offers nothing
Except unbroken misery. To live

14

From one day to the next on the verge of death,
Inching forward and back — can that give joy?
The man who is warmed by the glow of idle hope
Amounts to nothing. One of gentle birth
Has only one desire, a noble life
Or noble death. I have no more to say.

CHORUS:
Spoken like Ajax. No one could maintain
Those words did not ring true. But wait a little,   460
Put thoughts like these out of your mind, give up
Your settled purpose, let your friends persuade you.

TECMESSA:
Ajax, my master, there is no affliction
Harder to bear than the decree of fate.
I was the daughter of a freeborn father,
Powerful and rich, if any Phrygian was;
And now I am a slave. That, I suppose,
Was the gods' will; it surely was your doing.
I am concerned, then, since we live together,
For your well-being, and I beg of you   470
By Zeus who guards your hearthstone, by our union,
By the bed in which you made peace with your captive,
Not to expose me to your enemies'
Insults and mockery, or let me fall
Into a stranger's hands. The day you die,
Leaving me desolate, you may be certain,
Will be the day on which the Greeks will seize me
And drag me off to slavery with your son.
Then one of my new lords will speak of me
With insolence and contempt: "Ajax, the army's   480
Mightiest warrior, had that woman once.
Her life was happy then. Look at her now,
Doing a slave's work." They will talk like that.
Hardship will be my portion, but to you
And all your house such things will bring disgrace.
Reverence your father, Ajax. Do not leave him
Lonely, grieving, and old. Reverence your mother,
For she is old too, and she prays the gods
Time after time to bring you home in safety.
Pity your son, my lord, alone and friendless,   490
Under the care of guardians who can feel
No love for him. Think of the misery
That we two will inherit at your death.
I have nowhere to go, no one to ask to help me
Except for you. Your spear laid waste my land.
My parents are both dead; another fate
Has dragged them down to make their home in Hades.

15

I am left destitute, without a country.
You are all I have, and you alone can save me.
Give thought to me, even me. A man should cherish   500
The memory of all the happiness that was his.
Kindness calls forth more kindness. But if someone
Forgets the good that has been done to him,
Then true nobility is his no longer.

CHORUS:

If only you would pity her as I do!
You would admit that she has spoken well.

AJAX:

I will admit that she has spoken well
Once she has brought herself to do my bidding.

TECMESSA:

Dear Ajax, there is nothing I will not do.

AJAX:

Well then, bring me my son. I wish to see him.   510

TECMESSA:

I was afraid. I had him sent away.

AJAX:

When I was — in such distress? Is that your meaning?

TECMESSA:

Yes. The poor child. You might have seen and killed him.

AJAX:

It would have been in keeping. I am accursed.

TECMESSA:

That much at least I managed to prevent.

AJAX:

You have done well, Tecmessa. You showed foresight.

TECMESSA:

If that is so, how can I help you now?

AJAX:

Have him brought here to me, to see and speak to.

TECMESSA:

Yes, yes. He is close by. He is with the servants.

AJAX:

Then why am I kept waiting all this time?   520

TECMESSA:

My child, your father wants you. Bring him in
Whoever is in charge of him out there.

AJAX:

Is he ever coming? Did he hear you call?

TECMESSA:

Here is the man now, and the child is with him.

Enter a servant with EURYSACES

16

AJAX:

Up with him. Lift him up. Here in my arms.
The sight of fresh blood will not frighten him,
Not if he really is his father's son.
We must break him in at once, teach him to live
My rough, hard life, making my nature his.
Son, may you be the counterpart of your father,   530
Only more fortunate. Then you will prove
In no way base. Even now I envy you,
Untouched by all this misery around you,
For life is at its best when you feel nothing,
Before you learn what joy and sorrow are.
But when you do, see that my enemies know
The man you are, the man your father was.
Till then, let the soft breezes nourish you,
Enjoy your tender life that gives your mother
Such happiness. You may be sure no Greek   540
Will, in his hate, insult you or attack you,
Even if I am gone. I will leave Teucer,
Who will be tireless in his guardianship,
To care for you, though now he is far away,
Hunting his enemies down. My fellow sailors
Who have fought beside me, I assign to you
The task of sharing this kind-hearted service.
Let Teucer know he is to take this child
To my old father and mother to console them
And tend them during their remaining years.   550
Tell him this too: at the army's games, no judge —
Above all not the man who has destroyed me —
Is to award my armor as a prize.
Son, you are named for this, Eurýsacés.
Take this broad shield, spear-proof, seven ox-hides thick.
Hold it by the embroidered strap and wield it.
But have my other armor buried with me.
(*To* TECMESSA) Here is the child. Take him away at once,
And close the tent. Make sure you do not weep
In public here. Women are tearful creatures.   560
Be quick and shut it tight. A skillful doctor
Will not sing charms when he should use the knife.

CHORUS:

This eagerness of yours is frightening.
Your words have a cutting edge; they trouble me.

TECMESSA:

Ajax! My lord! What are you going to do?

AJAX:

No questions. Show a proper self-control.

17

TECMESSA:

You wring my heart. I beg you by our child,
By all the gods not to abandon us.

AJAX:

Stop being so persistent. Can you imagine
I owe the gods my service any longer?   570

TECMESSA:

Irreverence! Hush! AJAX: I am paying no attention.

TECMESSA:

You *will* not listen? AJAX: You have talked too much already.

TECMESSA:

Because I am frightened. AJAX: Shut the tent here. Quickly!

TECMESSA:

Let your heart soften! AJAX: You are a fool, I think,
If you are planning *now* to change my nature.

> *Exeunt* AJAX, TECMESSA, *and* EURYSACES *into the tent*

CHORUS:

O far-famed Salamis, forever happy,
　　Calm in the breaking seas, to all men dear!
We yet remember you in all our hardships,
　　　Worn out with lingering here
Quartered for endless months beside Mt. Ida,   580
　　　Holding this bleak hope fast:
That to the darkness of detested Hades
　　　We shall go down at last.

And now the curse the gods have inflicted on Ajax
　　Is a new burden that we must endure.
The mighty warrior whom you sent to battle
　　　Broods there alone, past cure,
A sorry spectacle for those who love him;
　　　While all the splendid things
He alone could have done are scorned and slighted   590
　　　By the two hateful kings.

Surely his mother, whom the years have silvered,
　　　Hearing of Ajax, will not wail
　　　　The ruin of his nature
In low tones like the plaintive nightingale.
No. She will cry out in wild lamentation,
　　In a loud burst of passionate despair,
　　　Raining down blows upon her bosom,
　　　　Tearing her hair.

Most nobly born of all the warriors, Ajax,   600
　　To his true self grown deaf and blind,
　　　Nurses his strange delusions.

Death would be better than a shattered mind.
What anguish will his wretched father suffer
   To learn of this disaster! for not one
      Of all his race has been so stricken
         Except *this* son.

Enter AJAX, *followed by* TECMESSA

AJAX:

Time in its mighty and unmeasured flow
Brings to light hidden things, and what is clear
Conceals in darkness. Man can think of nothing   610
That may not come to pass. The solemn oath,
The tough, unbending will are overborne.
For even I, keen-edged as tempered iron,
Feel myself softened by a woman's words,
And shrink from leaving her among my foes
Alone, with a fatherless child. But I will go
Down to the shore, and in the bathing-place
There in the meadows wash away these stains
To appease the grievous anger of the goddess.
Then I will take this sword, this hated weapon,   620
To some deserted place and bury it
Out of men's sight deep in the ground. And may
Darkness and Hades keep it there forever!
It was the gift of Hector, the most deadly
Of all my foes, and from the day he gave it
I have been shown no kindness by the Greeks.
How true the proverb is: an enemy's gift
Is not a gift, and brings no good with it.
From this day on I will obey the gods
And treat the sons of Atreus with respect.   630
They are our rulers and we must submit.
What else is there to do? Prerogative
Masters the mightiest and most awful powers.
For winter, blanketed with snow, gives place
To fruitful summer; night in his long, long rounds
Makes room for the white horses of the dawn,
Who comes enkindling light; the furious winds
Let the loud moaning sea subside in peace;
Even all-powerful sleep frees us at last,
He cannot always hold us prisoners.   640
And we — must we not learn self-discipline?
I will for one, for I have come to know
I should not hate my enemy so much
As to forget he will become my friend,
And I should help my friend but still remember
He will become my enemy in time.

19

Friendship for most men is a treacherous harbor.
No matter. For all this will turn out well.
Tecmessa, go inside and pray the gods
That my whole heart's desire may be fulfilled.   650

Exit TECMESSA

Friends, do as she has done. Respect my wishes.
Tell Teucer to take charge of my affairs
And be your friend as well. I take the path
That I must follow. But obey my orders,
And before long it may be you will hear
I have escaped from all my suffering.

Exit AJAX

CHORUS:
I soar aloft in my joy. I am shaken with sudden rapture.
    Come to us, Pan. Come over the sea.
        Come from the snow-swept mountain,
        The rocky slopes of Cylléné.   660
        I am longing to learn thy dances;
    O Pan, lord Pan, hear thou my plea.
        Great untaught king who teaches
        The gods to move in thy measures,
There are dances of Nysa and Cnosus. O Pan! Come
        dance them with me.
    And across the Icarian waters
    Phoebus Apollo, draw thou near.
    Show us thy favor, great lord of Delos.
        Appear! Appear!

I cry aloud. I rejoice. Fierce Ares, the god of bloodshed,   670
    Has lightened our cloud of consuming grief.
        O Zeus, on our swift-winged vessels
        Once more, once more the sunlight
        Can shine down brightly and purely.
    Ajax relents, his pain was brief,
        And humble and reverential
        He offers the gods their tribute.
The years are stronger than all; there is nothing beyond
        belief.
    What we dared not hope for has happened;
    His heart is softened, his anger past;   680
    His furious strife with the sons of Atreus
        Is ended at last.

Enter MESSENGER

MESSENGER:
    Friends, first of all, I have this news to give you.
    Teucer is back from Mysia, from the hills.

He had no sooner reached the generals' quarters
Than the whole army was insulting him.
When he was still far off, they saw him coming,
And when he got there, every man of them
Crowded around him, cursing and jeering at him.
He was the maniac's, the traitor's brother;   690
He never would escape; he would be stoned to death,
Smashed to a pulp. They even went so far
As to pull out their swords and hold them ready.
But when they had come to the very brink of fighting,
The old men intervened and quieted them.
But where is Ajax? I must tell him this.
He ought to know, for it concerns him most.

CHORUS:

He has gone away just now on some new business
That he has schooled himself to carry out.

MESSENGER:

Oh! Then the man who sent me here delayed   700
Too long, or I have been too long in coming.

CHORUS:

What was neglected that is so important?

MESSENGER:

Teucer instructed me to say that Ajax
Was not to leave his tent till he arrived.

CHORUS:

Well, he *has* left, and nothing could be better.
He has gone to appease the anger of the gods.

MESSENGER:

But you are talking nonsense, utter nonsense,
If Calchas can be trusted as a prophet.

CHORUS:

What did he say? What do you know about it?

MESSENGER:

I know this much. I happened to be near him.   710
During the council of the leaders, Calchas
Stepped to one side so that the sons of Atreus
Were out of hearing, greeted Teucer kindly,
Grasping him by the hand, and ordered him
To do his utmost to make Ajax stay
Inside his tent all day, and not to leave him
A single moment, if he wished to see him
Alive again. Only for this one day
Is he exposed to great Athena's anger.
"The gods send down," Calchas went on to say,   720
"Terrible suffering on the heads of those
Who growing overgreat amount to little,
And in their thoughts forget that they are human.

Ajax proved foolish when he first left home,
Unlike his father, who spoke sensibly.
'Go, son,' he said, 'and do your best to win,
But always with the help the gods can give you.'
'Father,' he answered in his arrogant folly,
'If the gods help him, anyone can succeed,
Even a man worth nothing. I intend   730
To win a glorious name without their help.'
That was the boast he uttered. And again,
When great Athena urged him on in battle,
Telling him to strike down his enemies
With his blood-stained hand, he answered her in words
Too blasphemous to be spoken: 'Goddess, stand
Beside the other Greeks, for where I am
No one will break our line.' Speeches like these,
Going beyond the limits set for men,
Provoked the terrible hatred of Athena,   740
But if he lives through this one day, perhaps
We may yet save him, if the gods are willing."
As soon as the prophet finished, Teucer rose
And sent me off to you with these instructions,
But if we find we cannot follow them,
Ajax is dead or Calchas has no skill.

CHORUS:
Tecmessa! Poor thing, you were born to suffer!
Come. Hear the news this messenger is bringing.
Disaster is too close to us for comfort.

                     Enter TECMESSA *with* EURYSACES

TECMESSA:
Why have you called me back? Just for a moment   750
I had found peace. What can have happened now?

CHORUS:
Listen to what this messenger will tell you.
We are alarmed by what he says of Ajax.

TECMESSA:
What *do* you say? Speak, man! Are we all ruined?

MESSENGER:
I did not hear *your* future. As for Ajax,
If he has left his tent, then I am anxious.

TECMESSA:
He has. Give me your news. You torture me.

MESSENGER:
Keep Ajax in his tent and do not let him
Go out alone. Teucer has sent those orders.

TECMESSA:
But where is Teucer? Why does he say such things?   760

MESSENGER:
>He has returned, and fears that some great danger
>Is threatening Ajax if he leaves his tent.

TECMESSA:
>How terrible! Who was it told him this?

MESSENGER:
>Calchas the prophet told him only now.
>Today brings either life or death to Ajax.

TECMESSA:
>Friends! Save me from the fate that threatens me.
>Run, some of you. Bring Teucer here at once.
>The rest of you go both ways, east and west,
>Along the shore. Search all the inlets. Find
>The fatal path he took. Now I can see 770
>My lord has tricked me. He had room for me,
>Once, in his heart; now he has banished me.
>Child, child, what shall I do? Not simply sit here.
>I will go myself, as far as I can. Come! Quickly!
>We cannot delay, if we intend to save
>A man who has gone in eager search of death.

CHORUS:
>I am ready now, to go not just to talk.
>You will see how quick I am, how fast I run.

>>>>TECMESSA *leaves* EURYSACES *in the tent
>>>>and exits with* CHORUS

The SCENE *changes to the seashore*

Enter AJAX. *He fixes his sword in its place near some
bushes. The hilt is buried in the ground, the blade is
pointing up*

AJAX:
>There is the killer where he cannot fail
>To do his work — if I have time enough 780
>For such reflections. It was Hector's sword,
>A token of his friendship, and I hated
>No one so much as him. It stands there fixed
>In the hostile soil of Troy, with a new edge
>Scoured by the whetstone. I have buried it
>Carefully; it will stand me in good stead
>As the means of quick death. I have done my part.
>And now, O Zeus, I call upon thee first,
>As I ought to do. Grant me my small request.
>Send thou some messenger with the news to Teucer 790

23

That he may be the first to lift me up
When I have fallen on this dripping sword,
Before some enemy catches sight of me
And throws me to the dogs and birds of prey.
Zeus grant me this. And next I pray to Hermes,
Our guide to the underworld, that he may spare me
The throes of death and lull me soon to sleep
When I have thrown myself upon this sword
In one swift leap. And I invoke the Furies,
The dread immortal maidens who stride far,   800
Watching forever all the woes of men:
Mark how the sons of Atreus have destroyed me;
Swoop down and seize them, crush them in utter ruin.
Come, ye swift-footed Furies! Glut your vengeance
On the whole army; let not one escape.
And thou, O Helios, whose chariot climbs
The steep slope of the heavens, when thou seest
My native land, tighten thy golden reins,
Tell my old father and my wretched mother
The tale of my calamities and my death.   810
Poor woman! When she hears such news as this,
She will cry out till the whole city rings
With her lament. But I accomplish nothing
By giving way to grief. I must not linger
In doing what I came to do. O Death!
Death! Draw thou near to me, come gaze upon me.
We shall still talk together, there as here.
But thou clear radiance that is shining now,
And thou great Helios in thy chariot,
I call to thee, this once, this one last time.   820
O light of day! O Salamis, my homeland,
The hallowed soil of my ancestral hearth!
O far-famed Athens, country of my kinsmen!
Farewell! And I salute you, rivers, springs,
And plains of Troy that nourished me. Farewell!
These are the last words Ajax speaks to you.
Henceforth he talks in Hades with the dead.

AJAX *falls on his sword out of sight behind the bushes*
Enter CHORUS *from left and right*

SEMI-CHORUS I:
  Search! Search! No end to our searching!
  Nowhere, nowhere
  We looked has he been seen or heard of.   830
  What was that? Listen!
S.-CH. 2: It is only the rest of us, only your shipmates.
S.-CH. I: What luck did you have?

24

S.-CH. 2:	We went to the west, on past the ships there.
S.-CH. 1:	What did you find?
S.-CH. 2:	That the going was rough — otherwise nothing.
S.-CH. 1:	He is not to be found on the eastern pathway,
	Of that we are sure.

CHORUS:

If only someone had seen him,
Wandering far in his fury —   840
Some fisherman toiling the whole night through,
Some nymph of the river or mountain —
    Who might give us a clue.
Ajax is sick and afflicted.
How hard it is that we,
Who have looked so long and gone so far to find him,
    Should fail so utterly.

TEC.: Oh! Oh!
CH.: What was that cry? There in the woods. Right there.
TEC.: Oh, no, no!   850
CH.: It is Tecmessa, the woman he won in battle.
    Poor creature! What a broken-hearted wail!
TEC.: (*entering*):   Friends, I am lost, undone, my life is wrecked!
CH.: What is it?
TEC.: Our Ajax has just died. Here is his body
    With the sword buried in it out of sight.
CH.:   There is no hope left! We shall never go back to
            our country.
        My lord, you have killed us too,
        The unfortunate men who have sailed here with
            you.
        And you, poor woman, we pity you.   860
TEC.: We can only weep for what has happened to him.
CH.: Poor man! Who did it? Whose hand struck him down?
TEC.: His own beyond all doubt. The sword he planted
    Here in the ground and fell on clearly proves it.
CH.:   What fools we were! We had no ears, no eyes!
            You died alone with no friend near to save you.
        We were utterly heedless. Show us where he lies,
            That stubborn man whose very name means sorrow.

TECMESSA:

I will not have him looked at. I will hide him
Under this mantle, cover him completely.   870
No one who loved him could endure the sight
Of the dark blood that gushes from his nostrils
And from the wound that he has dealt himself.
What shall I do? What friend will lift you up?
This is the time when Teucer should be here

To tend his brother's body. Oh, where is he?
Oh, Ajax! Ajax! To have fallen so low!
A sad sight even for your enemies.

CH.: Your life was doomed to destruction.
 By your railing against the Atridae,   880
Your bitter passion, your deadly hate.
 You were bound in the end, fierce spirit,
  To meet your fate.
Sorrow has followed sorrow
From the day the strife began,
With Achilles' golden armor to be given
 As the prize of the braver man.

TEC.: Oh, oh!
CH.: True and deep grief, I know, pierces the heart.
TEC.: Oh, oh!   890
CH.: It is no wonder you cry out, Tecmessa,
So lately robbed of one you loved so well.
TEC.: What you can guess at I feel all too deeply.
CH.: Yes, that is so.
TEC.: Son! Son! A yoke of slavery is ahead
For you and me, under hard taskmasters.
CH.: What you have said is terrible, Tecmessa.
 It would be an unspeakable thing
 If the sons of Atreus proved so cruel.
 May the gods avert such suffering.   900
TEC.: What we endured is what the gods have willed.
CH.: Yes. They have laid a crushing burden on us.
TEC.: This is the work of Zeus's dreadful daughter.
Athena caused this pain to please Odysseus.
CH.: Black-hearted, persistent man! He laughs and jeers,
 Exulting in all these evils, born of frenzy.
 And the two kings, when the story comes to their ears —
 It is bitter to think of! — join in his mocking laughter.

TECMESSA:
 Then let them laugh and triumph in his ruin.
 They felt no need of him while he was living.   910
 Now he is dead, perhaps in the thick of battle
 They will lament his loss. Stupid men never
 Can see they hold their own good in their hands
 Until they have thrown it away. His death has brought
 Less happiness to them than grief to me.
 To him it has brought joy. He longed for it.
 It was the comfort he has sought and found.
 Why should they laugh at him? They had no part
 To play in his death; that was the gods' concern.

26

Then let Odysseus have his empty triumph.
Ajax is dead. Nothing remains for them,
But he has left me anguish and lament.
TEUCER (*approaching*):
    Oh, dreadful!
CHORUS:
    Hush! I hear someone. Yes, it is Teucer's voice,
    And all our pain is in that cry of his.

                                        Enter TEUCER

TEUCER:
    Oh, Ajax, Ajax! My belovéd brother!
    What can have happened? Is the rumor true?
CHORUS:
    Yes, he is dead. That you must understand.
TEUCER:
    How can I bear it? It is bitter, bitter.
CHORUS:
    He is dead, Teucer. TEUCER: My heart aches for him.   930
CHORUS:
    You may well weep. TEUCER: How fierce an act! How
            sudden!
CHORUS:
    It was indeed. TEUCER: O misery! But where
    In this whole country will I find the child?
CHORUS:
    Beside the tent, alone. TEUCER: Then bring him quickly,
    Before some enemy snatches him away
    Like a lion's cub and leaves the lioness robbed.
    Go to him. Hurry. Do your part, Tecmessa.
    For men insult the dead who are lying helpless.

                                        Exit TECMESSA

CHORUS:
    Teucer, before he died he ordered you
    To guard the child, as you are doing now.   940
TEUCER:
    Never in all my life have I beheld
    So sad a sight. Never has any path
    So pierced my heart as this one, dearest Ajax,
    That led me here, trying to track you down
    The moment I had learned about your fate.
    For a swift rumor that you were dead and gone
    Swept through the army as if a god had sent it.
    When I first heard it, far from here, I managed
    To keep my groans low, but the sight of you
    Completely overwhelms me. Brother! Brother!   950

Take off that mantle. Let me see the worst.
A hard, stern face. Courage and cruelty.
You have sown a bitter harvest by your death
Which I must reap. What country can I go to?
What people will receive me, who have failed you
When you most needed me? How heartily
Our father Telamon will welcome me,
How brightly he will smile when I come home
Without you with me, he who never smiles
Even when things go well. There is no insult   960
That he will spare me. He will keep nothing back.
"You bastard, son of a slave I won in battle,
Coward, deserter, traitor," — to you, dear Ajax! —
"You hoped your trickery would win for you
His home and kingship after he was dead."
He will say things like that. He is hot-tempered,
And in his old age quick to take offense,
To quarrel over nothing. In the end
He will disown me and drive me from my country,
No longer free but railed at like a slave.   970
At home that is my future. Here at Troy
My enemies are strong and I am weak.
These are the profits that your death has brought me.
What shall I do? Oh, Ajax! can I lift
Your body from the blade of this bright sword
On which you died. Do you see now how Hector
After his death was fated to destroy you?
Think of the destiny of these two men!
Hector was dragged to death behind his chariot,
Bound to its rail by the same girdle Ajax   980
Had given him. And this is Hector's gift,
Fatal to Ajax, the sword he fell upon.
Did not a Fury hammer out the blade,
And Hades, that grim workman, make the girdle?
For my part, I believe the gods have always
Contrived the destinies of all mankind.
If someone disagrees, then let him rest
Contented with his view, as I with mine.

CHORUS:

No more, no more. Think of some way to make
A tomb for him, and think of how to answer   990
The enemy I see, coming perhaps
To mock our grief as every scoundrel does.

TEUCER:

Who is it? You see someone from the army?

CHORUS:

The man for whom we sailed here, Menelaus.

28

TEUCER:

> Yes. He is close enough to recognize.

> *Enter* MENELAUS *with two heralds*

MENELAUS:

> You there, you by the body! Keep your hands off.
> You are not to bury it. Leave it where it is.

TEUCER:

> Why have you spent your breath in such a speech?

MENELAUS:

> To give my orders, and our general's orders.

TEUCER:

> Is there some reason why you talk this way?　1000

MENELAUS:

> This reason. When we brought him here from Greece,
> We expected him to be our friend and ally,
> But we have found him a more deadly foe
> Than any Trojan, planning to destroy
> The whole Greek army with his murderous spear,
> Attacking us by night. If his attempt
> Had not been stifled by some god, his fate
> Would have been ours; we would be stretched out there
> In shameful death, and he would be alive.
> But a god turned his violence aside　1010
> So that it fell upon the sheep and cattle.
> And so I say there is no one in the world
> Powerful enough to give him burial.
> His body will be thrown on the yellow sands
> Somewhere, to feed the sea-birds. Stop! No threats,
> No blustering! We never could control him
> While he was still alive. He is now dead,
> And in our hands, whether or not you like it,
> And he will not rebel. During his lifetime
> He refused to listen to a word we said.　1020
> And yet the sure sign of an evil nature
> Is for a common man to set himself
> Against authority. A state can never
> Uphold the law when reverence is lacking.
> No army can be led and disciplined
> Without a bulwark of respect and fear.
> A man, however big, must not forget
> That he can fall, perhaps for a trivial reason.
> Fear and a sense of shame will keep him safe.
> The state that puts no curb on speech or action　1030
> May for a time sail with a favoring wind,
> But you may rest assured that in the end
> It will sink to the bottom. Fear should have a place

In the established order. How can we hope
To have our pleasures and not pay the cost
In sufferings? They come and go in turn.
This man was fiery and presumptuous once,
But *I* am arrogant now. Hear my command.
You are not to bury him, or you will find
You will need somebody to bury you.   1040

CHORUS:

Let these wise maxims, Menelaus, keep you
From insulting and dishonoring the dead.

TEUCER:

Friends, I will never be surprised again
If a common man behaves offensively,
When those of noble blood can let themselves
Utter such falsehoods. Come! Tell me again.
You say *you* brought him here? He was an ally
You found for the Greeks? He did not sail for Troy
As his own master? It was not his doing?
How are you *his* commander? By what right   1050
Are you the general of the men he brought
From his own home? You came as King of Sparta,
Not as our lord. Your power no more extended
To governing him than his to governing you.
You sailed here under orders. You were not
Captain of everyone including Ajax.
Rule your own people. Let them feel the lash
Of your proud words. But I will bury him
With all due honors, even if you forbid me,
You or that other general. What you say   1060
Will never frighten me. He went to war
Not for your wife's sake, like those wretched creatures
Your slaving subjects, but to keep the oath
That he had sworn — above all not for your sake.
Ciphers he disregarded. When you come back,
Bring some more heralds. Bring the commanding general.
I will not notice any noise you make
So long as you are the man that you are now.

CHORUS:

Harsh words are ill-advised in time of trouble.
Whether deserved or not they leave a wound.   1070

MENELAUS:

This bowman thinks quite highly of himself.

TEUCER:

Yes. There is nothing base in archery.

MENELAUS:

How you would boast if you had a warrior's armor!

TEUCER:

Without it, I could meet you fully armed.

MENELAUS:

    You show ferocious courage — in your talk.

TEUCER:

    In a just cause boldness may be forgiven.

MENELAUS:

    You think it just to give my murderer honors?

TEUCER:

    Murderer! Wonderful! You are alive and dead.

MENELAUS:

    Saved by the gods and dead in his intention.

TEUCER:

    Then if the gods have saved you, do not slight them.   1080

MENELAUS:

    How could I fail to reverence their laws?

TEUCER:

    By coming to stop the burial of the dead.

MENELAUS:

    The burial of an enemy is wrong.

TEUCER:

    Then Ajax had declared war openly?

MENELAUS:

    We hated one another. You know that.

TEUCER:

    He knew you robbed him, tampering with the votes.

MENELAUS:

    Not I. His failure was the judges' doing.

TEUCER:

    Fraud can be made to look like honesty.

MENELAUS:

    Someone is going to suffer for that speech.

TEUCER:

    No more, I think, than I make someone suffer.   1090

MENELAUS:

    I tell you this: that man shall not be buried.

TEUCER:

    This is my answer: I intend to do it.

MENELAUS:

    I saw a man once, a courageous talker,
    Urging his crew to sail in threatening weather.
    At sea, with the storm raging, you would find him
    Without a word to say, under his cloak
    For anyone to trample on who chose to.
    And you too, with your high and mighty language,
    May find a furious tempest springing up
    From a small cloud to silence all your uproar.   1100

TEUCER:

    And I once saw a man, an absolute fool,
    Insult his neighbors when they were in trouble.

Another man, someone resembling me,
Who felt as I do, looked at him and said,
"Do not abuse the dead, for if you do,
You can be certain you will suffer for it."
He looked him in the eye and warned the fellow.
It seems to me I see him. I am sure
You are the man. Have I been too obscure?

MENELAUS:

So. I am going. To stay here lecturing you   1110
Instead of using force would be disgraceful.

TEUCER:

Be off then! As for me, the worst disgrace
Is listening to such chatter from a fool.

> *Exit* MENELAUS

CHORUS:

A deadly quarrel is drawing near us.
Teucer, be quick. Be quick to find him
A hollow grave for his body to rest in,
A moldering tomb that men will honor,
Remembering Ajax in after ages.

> *Enter* TECMESSA *and* EURYSACES

TEUCER:

Look there! Ajax's wife and child are coming.
They are just in time to make the wretched body   1120
Ready for burial. Come here, my boy.
Stand by your father, put your hand on him,
And kneel down to implore him for his aid,
Holding three locks of hair — yours, hers, and mine,
The precious offerings of a suppliant.
If anyone should come here from the army
And drag you from the body, may he meet
A doom as terrible as his terrible deed:
May his unburied body be cast out
From his own country, and may all his race   1130
Be cut off root and branch, as I cut off
This lock of hair. Take it, my boy, and guard it.
Let no one move you. Kneel there and cling to him.
(*To* CHORUS) Stand next to him like men and not like
    women.
Help him till I get back. I will make ready
My brother's grave though all the world forbids it.

> *Exit* TEUCER

CHORUS:

Ah! When will the years be numbered of our far-distant
        roving?

When will they cease to be, the days of unending pain
That we have endured so long, the days of hardship and
    fighting,
  To the shame and sorrow of Hellas, here on the Trojan
    plain? 1140

I would that the man who taught us to league ourselves
    in warfare
  Had sunk to the depths of Hades or vanished into the
    air.
His was the savage strife by which our strife was be-
    gotten.
  It was he who wrought the destruction of all men
    everywhere.

  It was he, a man accursed, who robbed us
    Of every pleasure: love's delight,
  Garlands and wine-cups deep and brimming,
    And restful sleep at night.
For all that we know of Troy, of this dismal country,
  Is that here on our couches, with none to care, 1150
    Alone we lie, with the heavy dewfall
      Wetting our hair.

  Ajax sheltered us with his valor
    From nightly fears, from the darts of the foe.
  But now what joy in our lives is left us
    Since fate has brought him low?
Would we could sail past Sunium's level summit,
  Past the sea-washed headland's wooded height,
    Hailing the sacred land of Athens
      As it came into sight. 1160

              Enter TEUCER

TEUCER:
  I have hurried here, because I saw the general,
  King Agamemnon, coming, and I am sure
  He will pour out a torrent of abuse.
              Enter AGAMEMNON

AGAMEMNON:
  So you are the one. They tell me you have dared
  Rail at us and defy us, and have not yet
  Been punished — you, whose mother was a slave.
  Had she been nobly born, what arrogant speeches
  You would have uttered! With what haughty strides
  You would have walked the earth, when even now
  You, a mere nobody, have been defending 1170
  That nobody over there. You have maintained
  On oath that when we came here we were not

General or admiral of the Greeks, or you;
That Ajax sailed here independently.
Are we to hear such insolence from a slave?
Who was this man you boast about so much?
When did he lead a charge or stand his ground
When I was absent? In the whole Greek army
Was he the only man who could be found?
It seems the contest for Achilles' armor   1180
That we proclaimed is going to cost us dearly
If you are to keep accusing us of fraud,
Refusing to accept the judges' verdict,
A clear majority, that went against you;
If after losing you still slander us,
Still plot in secret how to injure us.
Under such circumstances law can never
Become established, when the rightful winners
Are thrust aside, when those who are in the rear
Are brought up to the front. That must be stopped.   1190
Broad-shouldered, brawny men are not the ones
Who are most dependable. Men who have brains
Always come out on top. A thick-ribbed ox
Is kept from straying by a little whip.
And that, I think, will be the course of treatment
You will be given unless you show more sense.
The man is dead, a shade, and you are still
Giving free rein to your impertinence.
Come to your senses. Remember who you are.
Go and get someone else, a free-born man,   1200
To plead your case. Your talk means nothing to me.
I cannot understand your foreign language.

CHORUS:
I can say only this: I wish you both
Would be more reasonable, more self-controlled.

TEUCER:
How short-lived is the gratitude of men,
How quickly it turns traitor to the dead,
If this man cannot find a word of tribute
To pay you, Ajax, you who spent yourself
In his behalf, who risked your life
Time and again. All that is tossed aside,   1210
All quite forgotten. (*to* AGAMEMNON) When you made
        just now
Your long ridiculous speech, had you forgotten
The time that you were penned inside your rampart,
Your army routed, your cause as good as lost,
The time he came alone and rescued you?

When the ships' quarterdecks were already blazing,
And Hector, leaping high across the trench,
Was nearing them, who staved off that disaster?
Was it not Ajax, who you say had never
Gone anywhere without your going with him?   1220
On that occasion did he do his duty?
Or was he faithful when he fought with Hector
In single combat, one of the volunteers
Who cast their lots into the crested helmet?
His was no lump of wet, reluctant earth,
But one that would be first to leap out lightly.
Those were the deeds he did, and by his side
I stood, a slave, the son of a foreign mother.
You scoundrel, what possessed you to abuse me
In just those terms? You know, of course, that Pelops,   1230
The founder of your house, your father's father,
Was a mere foreigner, a Phrygian;
That Atreus, who begot you, gave his brother
That most ungodly banquet where the father
Ate his sons' flesh. Your mother was a Cretan,
Whom her own father ordered put to death,
As food for the dumb fishes, when he found her
Topped by a lover. That is your descent.
How can you sneer at mine? I am the son
Of Telamon, and he was given my mother   1240
To share his bed as a reward for valor.
She was of royal blood, Laómedon's daughter,
The gift that Heracles, Alcmena's son,
Chose for my father. I am of noble blood,
Born of two noble parents. Does my speaking
Disgrace my kinsman's cause? Now that he lies there
Crushed by calamity, you feel no shame
In saying you will fling away his body
Unburied. If you do, you can be sure
That you will fling away our bodies with it,   1250
All three of them. To die when all men know
I die for Ajax will become me better
Than to die fighting for your wife — or is it
Your brother's wife? Take care, not for my sake
But for your own, for if you make me suffer,
You will regret that you were not a coward
Rather than so presumptuous to me.

Enter ODYSSEUS

CHORUS:
You have come just in time, my lord Odysseus,
If you have come to help, and not to hinder.

ODYSSEUS:

What is it, friends? I heard the angry voices   1260
Of the Atridae by this brave man's body.

AGAMEMNON:

Our angry voices! Yes, my lord Odysseus.
That foul-mouthed man has been abusing us.

ODYSSEUS:

How did that happen? I can pardon insults
If the man uttering them has been insulted.

AGAMEMNON:

He has been. But his conduct was atrocious.

ODYSSEUS:

What has he done to you? How has he harmed you?

AGAMEMNON:

He says he will perform the funeral rites
For that dead body there in spite of me.

ODYSSEUS:

Now will you let a friend speak frankly to you,   1270
And keep his right to work in harness with you?

AGAMEMNON:

Yes, certainly. I have not lost my senses.
I have no friend among the Greeks like you.

ODYSSEUS:

Then listen. For the love of all the gods,
Do not be savage. Do not fling away
This man unburied. Control your violence.
Hatred should not tread justice under foot.
He was my enemy as well as yours,
The worst in all the army, ever since
I won Achilles' armor. Even so,   1280
I never would refuse to do him honor
Or to acknowledge that he was the bravest
Of all the Greeks who ever came to Troy,
Except Achilles. You would be unjust
To be contemptuous of him. You would wrong
Not Ajax but the laws the gods lay down.
To injure a brave man when he is dead,
Even a man you hate, would be disgraceful.

AGAMEMNON:

You take his part against me, you, Odysseus?

ODYSSEUS:

Yes. Yet I hated him when it was right to.   1290

AGAMEMNON:

Should you not trample his dead body also?

ODYSSEUS:

A shameful victory ought not to please you.

AGAMEMNON:
> Piety is not easy for a king.

ODYSSEUS:
> When a friend gives good advice, he can accept it.

AGAMEMNON:
> A loyal man obeys authority.

ODYSSEUS:
> Be satisfied. Yielding to friends is triumph.

AGAMEMNON:
> Remember who it is you are befriending.

ODYSSEUS:
> He was my enemy, yet he was noble.

AGAMEMNON:
> What! You respect him, your dead enemy?

ODYSSEUS:
> For me, his worth outweighs his enmity.   1300

AGAMEMNON:
> You are the kind of man we call unsteady.

ODYSSEUS:
> Today's friends often are tomorrow's foes.

AGAMEMNON:
> So then, you think it right to make such friends?

ODYSSEUS:
> I do not think it right to be too stubborn.

AGAMEMNON:
> In this affair you make us seem like cowards.

ODYSSEUS:
> No. Upright in the eyes of all the Greeks.

AGAMEMNON:
> Then I am to permit this burial?

ODYSSEUS:
> You are, for I too will need burial sometime.

AGAMEMNON:
> Everyone works, I see, for his own interests.

ODYSSEUS:
> I do, at least. Should I work for someone else?   1310

AGAMEMNON:
> This must be called your doing, then, not mine.

ODYSSEUS:
> Just as you like. In any case be generous.

AGAMEMNON:
> You may be very sure that I would do
> Much more than this for you. But as for him,
> Both here on earth and in the world below
> I shall still hate him. You can please yourself.

Exit AGAMEMNON

CHORUS:

If anyone should say you were not wise,
Odysseus, he would show himself a fool.

ODYSSEUS:

I have this to tell you, Teucer. From now on
I am as great a friend as I was once   1320
An enemy. And I should like to join you
In burying your dead, sharing the burden
So that no duty which we owe the noblest
Of all our fellow men is left undone.

TEUCER:

I have only praise to give you, great Odysseus,
For words like those, showing me that my fears
Were utterly groundless. You alone stood by him,
His bitterest enemy among the Greeks.
Refusing to heap insults on the dead
Because you were alive, not like that crack-brained   1330
General, who arrived here with his brother
Intending to dishonor him, to cast
His body out unburied. May the Father
Who rules the heavens, the unforgetting Furies,
And Justice the avenger bring destruction
Upon those wicked men for having sought
To fling him out in undeserved disgrace.
Yet in the burial itself, Odysseus,
I hesitate to let you have a share.
That might displease the dead. But otherwise   1340
Join us by all means. If you wish to bring
Anyone from the army, he is welcome.
I will do all the rest. You have been kind
To us, Odysseus. Be assured we know it.

ODYSSEUS:

I would have liked to help, but I respect
Your feeling of reluctance. I will go.

Exit ODYSSEUS

TEUCER:

Come. We have lingered too long already.
Let us have done. Quickly, some of you,
Dig out his grave. *You* set the high caldron
Over the flames for the sacred cleansing.   1350
You go to the tent for his armor.
And you too, child, with what strength you can muster,
Gently take hold of your father, gently,
And help me lift him, for still through warm channels
Dark blood is flowing. Come, friends, all of you.

Let us lose no time in this great man's service,
Of all who have ever lived the noblest.

CHORUS:

Whatever things a man can see
He understands, but nothing more:
Not what his own fate is to be,   1360
Not what the future has in store.

The Women of Trachis

CHARACTERS IN THE PLAY

HERACLES

DEIANEIRA, *his wife*

HYLLUS, *their son*

LICHAS, *a herald*

NURSE

MESSENGER

AN OLD MAN

CHORUS *of women of Trachis*

CAPTIVES: *Iole and women of Oechalia*

ATTENDANTS

THE WOMEN OF TRACHIS

SCENE: *Trachis. Before the house of* HERACLES

Enter DEIANEIRA *followed by the* NURSE

DEIANEIRA:

There is a saying that has come down to us:
You cannot tell before a man has died
Whether his lot in life is good or bad.
But I know well, and I am not yet dead,
That mine is bitter and a burden to me.
While I still lived at Pleuron with my father,
Oeneus, no girl in all Aetolia shrank
From marriage as I did, because a river
Came as my suitor, the god Achelóus.
He took three forms to ask my father for me: 10
At times he was a bull, at times a serpent
Writhing and glittering, and at times a man
With a bull's head, from whose dark beard great streams
Of water flowed. Confronted with the prospect
Of such a husband, in my misery
I never ceased to pray that I might die
Before I reached his bed. Yet, to my joy,
Heracles came at last, the famous son
Of Zeus and of Alcmena, grappled with him,
And set me free. I cannot give details   20
Of how the struggle went. I do not know.
Someone who did not tremble at the sight
Might speak of it. But I was nearly driven
Out of my mind with terror as I sat there,
Lest in the end beauty should bring me sorrow.
Yet Zeus, the judge of battles, gave the contest
A happy ending — if it has been happy.
Heracles chose me for his wife. Since then
Never have I been free from deep misgivings
On his account. Night after anxious night   30
My troubles come and go. We have had children,
Whom he sees only as a farmer sees
A distant field, at seedtime and at harvest.
That was the life he led, returning home
Only to leave it, slaving for his master.
Now he has reached the end of all his labors,
Yet I have never been so apprehensive.
For since the killing of lord Iphitus

We have been exiles, living here at Trachis
In a stranger's house, while Heracles has gone, 40
No one can tell me where. I only know
He is away and I am in agony.
I am almost sure he has met with some mischance.
I have been waiting for a message from him,
Waiting in vain, for fifteen months. Yes, something
Fearful has happened, judging from that tablet
He gave me when he left me. I have often
Prayed to the gods it might not bring us harm.

NURSE:

My mistress Deianeíra, I have seen you
Before today lamenting for your husband 50
During his absence. Now, if it is proper
For slaves to give advice to those born free,
Then I may tell you what you ought to do.
Why not send off one of your many sons
To seek your husband? Hyllus would be best.
If he is anxious for his father's welfare,
He is the natural one for you to choose.
Look! There he is now, hurrying to the house,
And if you think my words were to the point,
You can make use of him as I suggested. 60

Enter HYLLUS

DEIANEIRA:

My dear child, someone humbly born, it seems,
Can utter words of wisdom, for this woman,
A slave, has spoken as a freeman speaks.

HYLLUS:

And how was that? Do you wish to tell me, mother?

DEIANEIRA:

When your father has been absent for so long,
It is shameful that you have not tried to find him.

HYLLUS:

But I *have* found him, if rumor can be trusted.

DEIANEIRA:

What is the rumor? Where do they say he is?

HYLLUS:

They say that all last year he has been working
In Lydia, for a woman, as her servant. 70

DEIANEIRA:

If he has borne that, anything can happen.

HYLLUS:

But I am told that he is now set free.

DEIANEIRA:

Where is he then? Is he alive or dead?

HYLLUS:

They say he is waging war on Eúrytus,
Lord of Euboéa, or is planning to.

DEIANEIRA:

Son, do you know that he has left with me
Trustworthy oracles of that very place?

HYLLUS:

No. I know nothing, mother. What do you mean?

DEIANEIRA:

They say that he will either meet his death there,
Or henceforth lead a life of happiness   80
Once he has brought this labor to an end.
Will you not help him, therefore, when his fate
Hangs in the balance? If he stays alive,
Then we are saved, or else we perish with him.

HYLLUS:

Yes mother, I will go. If I had known
About these oracles, I would have gone
Long before this. But as it was, my father
Was always so successful I could never
Feel much anxiety. Now that I know
I will do my utmost to find out the truth.   90

DEIANEIRA:

Then go, Hyllus. Something is gained by learning
That all is well, however late one learns.

Exit HYLLUS
Enter CHORUS

CHORUS:

O sun brought to birth by the night, despoiled of her
        starlight,
    And by the night in radiance laid to rest,
Where is Alcmena's son? We beg you to tell us,
        O blazing light.
        Through the narrow straits of the east does he journey,
    Or lean on the two pillars of the west?
    Speak, for no other can match your sight.

Deianeira's heart, we have heard, is filled with longing.   100
    She who was once in the olden days a prize
Men fought for, now like a suffering bird is lying
        On her lonely bed,
    Abandoned to her grief and haunted
With fear for her absent lord, her anxious eyes
    Fixed on the woe that lies ahead.

    Wave after wave rolls on across the ocean,
Blown by the north or the south wind's tireless breath.

So Heracles is lifted to the heavens,
Or dragged down to the depths of misery   110
By a life tumultuous as the Cretan sea.
    And yet some god stands ready to protect him,
Drawing him backward from the house of death.

    We speak with deference, yet in disapproval
Of your despondent mood, for you should learn
    Not to let hope be worn away to nothing.
Zeus the all-governing does not ordain
For any man a lifetime free from pain;
    But as the Bear wheels endlessly above us,
So joy and sorrow come to all in turn.   120

Neither starry night, nor riches, nor any affliction,
    Not one of them stays with us long, not one.
And others will find that grief and gladness
        Have a brief course to run.
Mistress, that is a truth you must remember.
    Zeus is his father. Will Zeus forget his son?

DEIANEIRA:
    You have come, I suppose, because you heard I suffered.
May *your* grief never teach you how my anguish
Consumes my heart. You cannot know it now.
A young thing grows apart, in innocence,   130
Where neither the sun's heat, nor sudden rain,
Nor any wind assails it, while it lives
A life of calm, untroubled happiness.
But when a maid is given the name of wife,
She is given her share of deep anxiety,
Night after night, for husband or for children.
A wife will understand the load I bear
From what she has experienced herself.
I have wept many times, but grief has never
Pierced me as it does now. Listen to this.   140
When my lord Heracles on his last journey
Was leaving home, he gave me an old tablet
Inscribed with characters which he had never
Been willing to explain to me before,
However often he had started out
For some great struggle. He had always gone
As if he meant to triumph, not to die.
This time he spoke like one no longer living:
I was to take my widow's dower; his sons
Were to be given their portions of his lands.   150
He fixed the time for this by telling me
That a year and three months after he had gone
Would be the fateful time — and it has come —

When he would die or live on happily
Once he survived this crisis. That, he said,
Would end his labors, that was the gods' decree
He had heard years ago, when at Dodona
The ancient oak pronounced the oracle
Through the lips of the two priestesses, the Doves.
And now the very moment has arrived   160
For the fulfillment of the prophecy,
So that I start up from my pleasant sleep
Aghast to think that I may have to live
Without the noblest man in all the world.

CHORUS:

Do not say such grievous things. Here comes a man
Whose wreath of laurel shows he brings good news.

Enter MESSENGER

MESSENGER:

Madam. I am the first to give you news
That will end all your fears. He is alive.
Heracles is victorious, and brings back
The spoils of battle for our country's gods.   170

DEIANEIRA:

What did you say, old man? What did you say?

MESSENGER:

You will soon see your husband, praised and honored,
Coming in all the glory of his triumph.

DEIANEIRA:

What citizen or stranger told you that?

MESSENGER:

Lichas, the herald, is announcing it
To the crowd in the summer pasture. When I heard him,
I hurried here to be the first to tell you.
Frankly, I hoped for some reward or thanks.

DEIANEIRA:

But why not come himself, if his news is good?

MESSENGER:

He had no chance to, madam. All the Malians   180
Are showering him with questions, pressing round him
So that he cannot move. They are all eager
To learn what happened and will not let him go
Until they are satisfied. He is kept there
By what *their* wishes are, not by his own.
However, you will see him before long.

DEIANEIRA:

O Zeus, great lord of Oeta's unreaped fields,
Thou hast sent us happiness at last. Lift up
Your voices, women, here and in the house.

This news is like dawn breaking. Let us gather 190
The harvest of a joy we could not hope for.

CHORUS:

    Rejoice, rejoice for this house, you maidens! Raise
      Your song of triumph there by the fireside,
      While the chorus of men cry aloud in praise
      Of Apollo who bears the bright quiver,
        The god who defends us.
      And let all the maidens here
    Sing together, sing to his sister,
Ortýgian Artemis, goddess who holds the twin torches,
      The huntress of deer. 200
    And sing to the nymphs her neighbors.
I cannot reject you, O flute, you are lord of my spirit;
    Your music calls, and I rise and follow.
      The ivy has caught me in its embrace,
    Whirling me round in a Bacchanal frenzy.
      Hail to the Healer! Hail to Apollo!
    See, dear mistress, good news in person.
      There! You are face to face.

DEIANEIRA:

    Yes, yes, dear friends. I have been keeping watch
    And could not fail to notice all those people. 210

        Enter LICHAS *and the captive women*

    Welcome at long last, herald, if in truth
    The message you are bringing us is good.

LICHAS:

    We are happy, madam, to have come and heard
    Words that befit the occasion, for a man
    Who has triumphed should indeed be warmly welcomed.

DEIANEIRA:

    Good friend, tell me this first. I have to know
    This first — shall I see Heracles alive?

LICHAS:

    Certainly when I left him he was living,
    Rugged and vigorous, in perfect health.

DEIANEIRA:

    Is he in Greece or in a foreign country? 220

LICHAS:

    He is building Zeus an altar in Euboea,
    At Cape Cenaéum, to give him his first fruits.

DEIANEIRA:

    Was this because of an oracle or a vow?

LICHAS:

    A vow, made when he undertook to ravage
    The country of these women you see here.

DEIANEIRA:

Ah, these! Who are they? Whom do they belong to?
Unless I am wrong, their lot is pitiable.

LICHAS:

They are slaves he chose for himself and for the gods
When he destroyed the city of Eurytus.

DEIANEIRA:

Has he been fighting that campaign for all   230
This inconceivable time, these countless days?

LICHAS:

No, madam. He was kept in Lydia
Most of the time, no free man, so he says,
But a bought slave. That word should not offend you
When slavery is clearly Zeus's doing.
Purchased by Ómphalé, a barbarian,
He spent, he says, a whole year in her service;
And the disgrace so stung him that he swore
A solemn oath by which he bound himself
To enslave the man, with all his family,   240
Who had made him suffer. He did not swear in vain.
When his sin at last was purged, he raised an army
Of mercenaries and attacked the city
Of Eurytus, the only man, he said,
Responsible for what he had undergone.
For Eurytus, with his old friend Heracles
A guest at his own hearth, heaped insults on him
With deadly malice. "What if you do have arrows
That never swerve?" he said: "My sons are archers
Who would make short work of you in any contest."   250
"You are a freeman's broken slave," he cried.
And at a feast, when Heracles was drunk,
He threw him out of the house. This so enraged
Heracles that one day when Iphitus
Came to the hill of Tiryns on the track
Of his lost horses, Heracles caught the man
Looking away in an unguarded moment,
And hurled him from the flat top of the ramparts.
Angered by such a deed, Olympian Zeus,
Father of all mankind, had Heracles   260
Sold as a slave and banished without pity,
Because for once he had used trickery
To kill a man. Had his revenge been open,
Zeus surely would have pardoned that just triumph,
For the gods, like us, hate insolence. So all
Those arrogant men with their abusive tongues
Dwell in the mansion of the dead. Their city
Has been enslaved. The women you see here,

Their happy lives reduced to misery,
Have come to you. That was your husband's order, 270
Which I, his loyal servant, have obeyed.
And as for him, you certainly will see him
When he has given Zeus, god of our fathers,
A votive offering for his victory.
And that indeed, of all these happy tidings,
Is the most welcome word that you could hear.

CHORUS:

Mistress, your happiness is clearly shown
In what you see and what you heard him promise.

DEIANEIRA:

Yes, I have every reason to rejoice
At news like this, news of my lord's good fortune. 280
Rejoicing and success go hand in hand.
Yet if we stop to think, our minds misgive us
Because we know success may end in ruin.
My friends, how pitiful it is to see
These wretched exiles, homeless, fatherless,
Adrift in a strange land, perhaps the daughters
Of free-born fathers, but now forced to live
A life of slavery. O Zeus, who givest
Victory in battle, I pray thee deal not harshly
With any child of mine, or if thou wilt 290
Not while I live. My heart is filled with fright
When I see these women here. (*To* IOLÉ) Poor child,
who are you?
Unmarried, or a mother? You are noble
To judge by your appearance, and have never
Known such disgrace before. Lichas, who is she?
Who was her mother? Who was her father? Tell me.
I pity her the most, for she alone
Feels the full weight of her calamity.

LICHAS:

How should I know? Why do you ask? Perhaps
Her house is not the humblest in the country. 300

DEIANEIRA:

The royal house? Did Eurytus have a daughter?

LICHAS:

I do not know. Questions were not my business.

DEIANEIRA:

You did not hear her name from someone with her?

LICHAS:

Never. I did my work and I kept still.

DEIANEIRA:

Well then, poor girl, tell me your name yourself.
Not to know who you are distresses me.

LICHAS:

If she speaks now, that will be something new,
You may be sure. So far she has not said
A single word of any kind. Poor creature,
There has not been a moment since she left   310
Her wind-swept home that she has not been struggling,
With bitter tears, under her weight of sorrow.
Her lot is harsh, but we should show forbearance.

DEIANEIRA:

Let us spare her then. Let her go in the house
Just as she pleases. She ought not to suffer
On my account more than she suffers now.
She has enough to bear. Let us all go in.
Then you will lose no time in starting off,
And I will make things ready in the house.

Exeunt LICHAS *and the captive women*
MESSENGER *stops* DEIANEIRA

MESSENGER:

Stay here a minute first, now they have gone,   320
And let me tell you whom you sent inside,
For there is something you have not been told
That you should hear. And I know all about it.

DEIANEIRA:

What is it then? Why do you keep me here?

MESSENGER:

Wait. Listen. What I said at first has proved
Worth listening to, and so, I think, will this.

DEIANEIRA:

Shall I call the others back, or do you want
To talk to me and to these women here?

MESSENGER:

To you and them as well — not to the others.

DEIANEIRA:

You see, they are gone. Now you can tell your story.   330

MESSENGER:

You cannot trust a word that man has uttered.
Either what he said now was not straightforward,
Or else his first report was all a lie.

DEIANEIRA:

What do you mean? I do not understand
What you have said. You must explain more clearly.

MESSENGER:

I heard that man — and there were many others
Who heard him also — say that Heracles
For that girl's sake killed Eurytus, and destroyed
High-towered Oechália; and that he was driven

To all this violence by the spell of Eros, 340
Not by some other god, or by the way
He toiled as Ómphalé's slave in Lydia,
Or by his hurling Iphitus to his death.
But in this new account love is kept hidden.
The fact is, when he could not get her father
To give the girl to him to share his bed,
He made some trivial complaint the pretext
For launching an attack upon her country.
He killed the king and sacked the city. Now
He is coming home, and as you see, has sent her 350
On to this house, not carelessly, and not
As a mere slave. Do not imagine that.
It is most unlikely, madam, when his heart
Is hot with love. And so I thought it best
To tell you everything I heard him say.
He spoke in public. All the men of Trachis
There in the crowd heard him as well as I did,
And can convict him also. I am sorry
If my words pain you, but I speak the truth.

DEIANEIRA:
What awful thing has happened? What have I done? 360
Welcomed a hidden enemy to my home!
I cannot bear to think of it. The man
Who brought her here swore she was nameless. Is she?

MESSENGER:
She has a great name and is nobly born.
She is the child of Eurytus. They called her
Íolé. But of course he could not tell you
About her parentage. He never asked!

CHORUS:
Beyond all other scoundrels may that man
Be cursed whose acts are base and treacherous.

DEIANEIRA:
Friends, tell me! What am I to do? The news 370
I have just heard dismays me utterly.

CHORUS:
Go and ask Lichas. He might tell the truth
If you persisted in your questioning.

DEIANEIRA:
I will indeed. That seems like good advice.

MESSENGER:
Can I do more for you? Shall I stay here?

DEIANEIRA:
Yes. There he comes now of his own accord
Out of the house, without my sending for him.

Enter LICHAS

LICHAS:
>Give me my orders, madam. What do I say
>To Heracles? You see that I am starting.

DEIANEIRA:
>You came so slowly. How quickly you rush off   380
>Without allowing time for further talk!

LICHAS:
>My time is yours if you have any questions.

DEIANEIRA:
>Will you be honest? Will you tell the truth?

LICHAS:
>By great Zeus, yes — as much truth as I know.

MESSENGER:
>Then tell me this. Who is the girl you brought here?

LICHAS:
>She is Euboean. I do not know her parents.

MESSENGER:
>Look here! Whom do you think you are talking to?

LICHAS:
>Look here yourself! Why do you ask me that?

MESSENGER:
>You had better answer if you have your senses.

LICHAS:
>I am speaking to the lady Deianeira,   390
>Daughter of Oeneus, wife of Heracles,
>Unless my eyes deceive me, and my mistress.

MESSENGER:
>I wanted to hear that, that very thing.
>You say she is your mistress? LICHAS: Yes, of course.

MESSENGER:
>Then what if you are false, and are found guilty?
>What punishment will you deserve for that?

LICHAS:
>If I am false? Is this some trick or other?

MESSENGER:
>Not mine. The trickery is all your doing.

LICHAS:
>What a fool I have been to listen! I am off.

MESSENGER:
>No. Not before you answer one short question.   400

LICHAS:
>Ask what you want. You cannot be called tongue-tied.

MESSENGER:
>About that girl you brought here as a captive,
>You know the one? LICHAS: Yes. Why do you ask?

53

MESSENGER:
> You said this girl you now know nothing of
> Was Íolé, the child of Eurytus.

LICHAS:
> To whom did I speak? Is anyone going to come here
> To say he heard a thing like that from me?

MESSENGER:
> You spoke to many citizens of Trachis,
> A large crowd heard you say as much in public.

LICHAS:
> They may have given that as their impression —   410
> A different thing from an exact account.

MESSENGER:
> Impression! When you stated, under oath,
> You brought her as a bride for Heracles?

LICHAS:
> I brought her as a bride! By all the gods,
> Dear mistress, tell me who this stranger is.

MESSENGER:
> Someone who heard you say that love for her
> Laid the whole city waste. The Lydian woman
> Was not the cause, but passion for this girl.

LICHAS:
> Let him go, mistress. No one who is sane
> Wastes his time arguing with a lunatic.   420

DEIANEIRA:
> By Zeus whose lightning flashes through the glens
> High on the slopes of Oeta, I implore you
> Keep nothing back from me. You will not find me
> Naïve or bitter, I who know how wayward
> Human affection is. It would be folly
> To try to face love and trade blows with him.
> Love works his will upon the gods, and me.
> Why not some other woman such as I am?
> So then, I would be mad to blame my husband,
> Afflicted as he is with this disorder,   430
> Or to blame her, his partner in a thing
> That neither shames them nor does harm to me.
> Never! I could not do it. But if he taught you
> To tell a lie, you learned a wicked lesson.
> Or if you taught yourself, you will prove cruel
> Even if you intended to be kind.
> Tell me the truth. A free man is disgraced
> When he is branded with the name of liar.
> If you suppose you can escape detection,
> Many have heard you speak, and they will tell me.   440

And if you are afraid, your fear is groundless.
Not to know everything would pain me deeply.
To know — how is that shocking? Heracles
Before today has taken many women —
No man has taken more — but none of them
Has had to bear my insults or reproaches;
Nor will this girl, not even if her soul
Were steeped in love. Indeed, I pitied her
Deeply, poor creature, when I saw her first,
Because her beauty has laid waste her life,   450
And in all innocence she has brought destruction
And slavery on her city. Well, all that
Is past and done with now. But as for you,
I say again: lie, if you wish, to others
But do not fail to speak the truth to me.

CHORUS:

  Well said. Obey her. You will have no cause
  To regret it later, and will earn our thanks.

LICHAS:

  Well then, dear mistress, since I see you know
  Our human destiny and can make allowance
  For human weakness, I *will* tell the truth   460
  And keep back nothing. What this man has said
  Is true. It was because of this girl here
  That Heracles was driven wild with love,
  And that Oechalia, her unhappy country,
  Was leveled by his spear. To do him justice,
  He never said I was to keep it secret,
  Never denied it. As for me, dear madam,
  I was afraid my story would distress you.
  And if you think this wrong, I have done wrong.
  But now that you have learned the truth, be kind. 470
  Bear with her, both for his sake and your own,
  And make sure that you always will be guided
  By what you have said of her; for Heracles,
  Victorious in everything but this,
  Has been enslaved by passion for the girl.

DEIANEIRA:

  That is precisely what I mean to do.
  I will not fight against the gods in vain.
  I have enough to bear. Come in with me
  And get my messages. And you must take
  The gifts I owe you in exchange for yours.   480
  You brought along so many followers
  It is not right to have you leave with nothing.

       Exeunt DEIANEIRA *and* LICHAS

> Ever triumphant is she,
> The Cyprian, great Aphrodite.
> I do not speak of the gods, or tell how she caught in
> her snare
> The son of Cronus, and Hades, lord of the dark, and
> earth-shaking
> Poseidon, lord of the sea.
> But when our mistress was courted, who came as her
> suitors,
> And struggled to win her hand? What mighty pair
> Met with a hail of blows in the blinding dust of battle?   490

> From Óeniadaé came one,
> The river-god, great Achelóus,
> In the shape of a four-footed bull, high-horned, a ter-
> rible sight.
> And the other came from Thebes, a city beloved of
> Bacchus,
> Heracles, Zeus' son,
> With a springing bow, and spears, and a club that he
> brandished.
> Aflame for a bride, they rushed together to fight,
> And the goddess of marriage joy was standing beside
> them as umpire.

> Then the noise of struggle arose —
> The thudding of fists, the twang of a bow, deep
> groaning,   500
> A bull's horns clashing, the deadly blows
> Of a butting head — as the two of them twisted and
> grappled,
> And the girl in her delicate beauty
> On a far-off hill awaited her future husband.
> Thus it was that they fought, while the lovely bride,
> The prize of the battle, watched for the end in anguish.
> Then all at once from her mother's side
> She was gone, like calf forsaken.
>   *Enter* DEIANEIRA *with a servant carrying a box*

DEIANEIRA:

> Dear friends, our visitor is in the house
> Bidding good-bye to the captive women there;   510
> So I have stolen outside, partly to tell you
> What I have just contrived to do, and partly
> To have you join with me in my lament.
> A girl has come to me — no, an experienced woman —
> And I have taken her in, the way a seaman

56

Takes in his cargo, freight that will wreck my peace.
For now we two await the same embraces
Under the same sheet. This is the reward
My true and virtuous husband, Heracles,
Has given me, who have kept a home for him   520
Through all these weary years. I am not angry,
I cannot be, for he has often suffered
From the same sickness. But to live together
Beneath one roof, sharing one marriage with her —
What woman could endure that? I can see
That her young beauty is about to bloom,
While mine is fading. Men gaze eagerly
At a fresh blossom, and they turn away
When it is withered. And so I am afraid
He will be called my husband but in fact   530
Will be her lover, for she is younger. Still
As I have said, no woman who has good judgment
Gives way to anger. Dear friends, let me tell you
The remedy that may bring me some relief.
For years I had a gift that I kept hidden
In a bronze urn, a gift a centaur gave me,
The hairy-chested Nessus. As a girl
I took it from his wounds when he was dying.
He levied toll for carrying men across
The deep flood of the Evenus in his arms,   540
With neither oar to help him nor a sail.
I too was carried over on his shoulders,
When first my father sent me off to follow
Heracles as a wife, but in mid-stream
His lewd hand touched me and I shrieked. At once
Heracles turned and sent an arrow hissing
Into his breast that pierced him through the lungs.
Then, at the point of death, he said to me:
"Daughter of Oeneus, listen, and you will find
That being the last of all my passengers   550
Will stand you in good stead. Collect the clotted
Blood from my wounds, dark with the Hydra's gall,
The Lernéan monster, in which Heracles
Has dipped his arrows. It will prove to be
A charm that will prevent his ever seeing
Anyone else whom he will love more dearly
Than he loves you." Friends, it was this I thought of.
After his death I kept it locked away.
Now I have dipped this robe here (*indicating the box*)
                    in the blood
Just as he told me to before he died.   560
So it is ready. I am not rash or wicked

Even in thought. May I never learn to be,
For I despise a woman who stoops so low.
Yet if a spell or charm to win his love
Gives me some hope of conquering this girl,
I am prepared to use it, unless you think
That I am reckless. If so, I will do nothing.

CHORUS:

Provided you have grounds for confidence,
We do not think that such a plan is wrong.

DEIANEIRA:

Confidence? Well, there seem to be good prospects.　　570
I have not tested them. I have no proof.

CHORUS:

You have to act in order to be sure.
Without experience you can only guess.

DEIANEIRA:

We shall soon know. I see the man already
There at the door, about to leave. Be careful
Not to betray me. What is done in secret,
Even if shameful, will not bring disgrace.

Enter LICHAS

LICHAS:

What is your wish? Give me your orders, madam.
I have already stayed beyond my time.

DEIANEIRA:

I have been getting ready for you, Lichas,　　580
While you were inside, talking to the women.
Here is a gift, the work of my own hands,
For Heracles, a finely woven tunic.
And when you give it him, be sure to tell him
That he himself must be the first to wear it,
That he must not expose it to the sunlight,
Or to a holy precinct's altar flame,
Or to a glowing hearth, until he lets
The gods behold it as he stands before
The people on a day of sacrifice.　　590
For I had vowed that if I ever saw
Or learned beyond doubt he was safely home,
I would have him wear this tunic and appear
Clad in new clothes, to do the gods new service.
And to confirm my message take him this,
My seal (*on the box*), which he will recognize at once.
Now go. Take care to keep in mind the rule
That messengers should not exceed their orders.
Then my thanks will be added to my husband's,
Doubling the gratitude that you will earn.　　600

58

LICHAS:
> If I have any knowledge of my calling,
> The art of Hermes, I will make no slip.
> I will deliver this just as it is,
> And to explain it, will repeat your message.

DEIANEIRA:
> Then you had better leave me, for you know
> How matters stand with us, here in the palace.

LICHAS:
> I do. I will report that all goes well.

DEIANEIRA:
> And you saw too how I received the girl?
> You understand that she was treated kindly?

LICHAS:
> I was amazed. It moved me deeply, madam.   610

DEIANEIRA:
> What is there left to say? I am afraid
> It is too soon to speak about my love
> When I am not yet sure that I am loved.
>
> *Exeunt* LICHAS *and* DEIANEIRA

CHORUS:
> All ye who dwell by the heights of Oeta
>   Where the hot springs gush from the rocks; and ye
> Who dwell by the shore of the sheltered roadstead,
>   The inmost reach of the Malian sea,
> By the shore beloved of the maiden goddess,
>   Artemis armed with her arrows of gold;
> Who dwell in the land where the Greeks at Pylae   620
>   Their far-famed council hold,
>
> Soon, soon, neither harsh nor grieving,
>   The glorious notes of the flute will rise
> As piercing sweet as the lyre's music,
>   The heavenly strains the immortals prize,
> For the son of Zeus is at last returning.
>   Heracles whom Alcmena bore,
> Laden with spoils of all his triumphs,
>   Is hastening home once more.
>
> He was lost to us, lost as he roamed through the sea,   630
> While we waited for twelve long months and heard nothing,
>   And his faithful wife in her misery
> Wasted away with her endless weeping.
>   Now Ares, maddened, has set her free,
> Putting an end to her days of sorrow.

May he come, may he come! Do not rest, do not tire,
O many-oared ship that carries him hither.
    May he leave the island's altar-fire
Where they say he stands, and come to our city
    Fresh from the sacrifice, steeped in desire,   640
Subdued by the spell she learned from the centaur.

> *Enter* DEIANEIRA

DEIANEIRA:

I am afraid, my friends, afraid I may
Have gone too far in what I did just now.

CHORUS:

What is the matter? What has happened, madam?

DEIANEIRA:

I am not sure, but I have grave misgivings.
My good intentions may have done great harm.

CHORUS:

You cannot mean your gift to Heracles?

DEIANEIRA:

I do. And I say this: no one should act
Too eagerly when he is acting blindly.

CHORUS:

Why are you frightened? Tell us, if you will.   650

DEIANEIRA:

If I tell you what has happened, you will hear
Something so monstrous no one could have dreamt it.
The tuft of soft, white wool I used just now
To smear the robe has vanished, not destroyed
By anything in the house but by itself.
It has been eaten from within and now
Is crumbled into dust. But I must tell you
All the details so you may know exactly
What has occurred. I have neglected none
Of the instructions that were given me   660
By the savage centaur as he lay in pain,
Pierced by the arrow. They were like words
Indelibly engraved on a bronze tablet,
And I have heeded them. I was to keep
The ointment safely hidden in the house
Away from fire, away from the heat of the sun
So that whenever I might want to use it
I could apply it freshly. I obeyed.
Then, when I had to act, I smeared the robe,
Inside the house, in secret, with soft wool,   670
A tuft I pulled from one of the household sheep.
No sun had touched my gift. I folded it,
And laid it in a box, as you have seen.

But when I left just now, I saw a sight
Beyond description, beyond all comprehension.
I happened to have thrown the scrap of wool
I smeared the robe with where the sun beat down
Directly on it. As the wool grew warm,
It shriveled up and crumbled into powder
Like sawdust when a log of wood is cut.   680
There it is lying where I threw it down,
But from the earth on which it was exposed
Foam thick and clotted has come bubbling up,
Like rich, new wine poured out upon the ground,
Juice of the blue grapes of the vines of Bacchus.
And so I am bewildered, desperate!
I only know I have done something fearful.
What reason could that dying monster have
To show me kindness, when I caused his death?
None, none! He tricked me so that he could kill   690
The man who shot him. I have learned the truth
Too late for it to be of any help,
For I am sure, unless my dread misleads me,
That I alone — how awful! — shall destroy him.
I know the deadly arrow wounded even
Cheiron, a god. I know that it is fatal
To every beast it touches. Can this venom,
This black blood welling from the wound of Nessus,
Fail to kill Heracles? No, no, it cannot!
However, this is certain: if he falls,   700
I will go down beneath the same disaster.
No woman could endure an evil name
Whose dearest wish is to be held in honor.

CHORUS:
> Terrible things are certainly to be feared,
> But we should not lose hope till they occur.

DEIANEIRA:
> How can you hope when you have acted wrongly?
> Nothing is left to give you confidence.

CHORUS:
> But when the wrong is unintentional,
> Men grow less angry, as they should with you.

DEIANEIRA:
> Those who are not involved may talk that way,   710
> Not those who have had a share in any wrong.

CHORUS:
> It would be better to say nothing more,
> Unless you want to tell it to your son.
> Hyllus is here, who went to find his father.

Enter HYLLUS

HYLLUS:
    Oh mother, how I wish that you were dead,
    Or not *my* mother but some other man's,
    Or changed to someone different, someone better!
    If only one of these three things were true!

DEIANEIRA:
    Hyllus, what have I done to make you hate me?

HYLLUS:
    What have you done? Listen to what I tell you.   720
    Today you killed your husband, my own father.

DEIANEIRA:
    Oh Hyllus, Hyllus! What is that you said?

HYLLUS:
    I told the truth, for when a thing has happened,
    What man can ever do away with it?

DEIANEIRA:
    How can you speak so, Hyllus? Who has told you
    That I have done so dreadful a thing as that?

HYLLUS:
    No one has told me. I do not speak from hearsay.
    I saw my father's fate with my own eyes.

DEIANEIRA:
    You found him? You were with him? Where was that?

HYLLUS:
    If you must hear, I must tell everything.   730
    After the sack of Eurytus' famed city,
    He carried off the trophies and the finest
    Spoils of the victory. On the Euboean coast
    There is a sea-washed headland, Cape Cenaeum,
    Where he marked out a grove and set up altars
    Sacred to Zeus, our fathers' god; and there
    I had the joy of seeing him at last.
    He was about to sacrifice, to make
    A splendid offering, when his herald, Lichas,
    Arrived from home here with your fatal gift.   740
    He put the robe on as you told him to,
    And then, starting with twelve unblemished bulls,
    The pick of all the spoil, he brought to the altar
    A hundred victims, a mixed herd of cattle.
    At first, poor wretch, he prayed, serene and happy,
    Pleased with his handsome robe. But when the flame
    Began to spring up, fed by the resinous pine
    And by the blood from the holy sacrifice,
    He broke into a sweat, and the robe clung
    Close to his sides, moulded to every joint   750
    Like sculptor's work. Pain, gnawing at his bones,

Pierced through him, when some cruel venom, deadly
As a viper's poison, started to devour him.
At that, he shouted for the unfortunate Lichas,
Who had no share at all in your wrongdoing,
Accusing him of treachery in bringing
That robe to him. But he, poor man, knew nothing,
And answered that the gift was yours alone,
That he had brought it just as you had sent it.
When he heard these words, my father was convulsed   760
With rending agony that clutched his lungs,
And seizing Lichas by the ankle, hurled him
Against a rock that jutted from the sea
So that the white brains oozed out from his hair,
And the blood spattered from his broken skull.
The people gave a cry of awe and grief,
Seeing one frenzied and the other dead,
But no one dared approach him. Spasms of pain
Dashed him to the earth or flung him in the air,
Shrieking and screaming till the rocks re-echoed,   770
The high, steep headlands of Locris, the hills of Euboea.
But when he was spent from throwing himself on the ground
Time and again, crying aloud in his anguish,
Cursing his ill-matched marriage to a wretch
Such as you are, the match that Oeneus granted,
That had destroyed his life, he raised his eyes,
Distorted, from the smoke that swirled around him,
And seeing me in the great crowd, bathed in tears,
Called out to me, "Hyllus, my son, come here.
Do not forsake me in my agony,   780
Even if you must die as I am dying.
Take me away, and the best place for you
To put me down is where no man can see me.
Or if you pity me too much for that,
At any rate be quick and carry me
Out of Euboea. Keep me from dying here."
At this command we laid him in a ship,
And have contrived to land him in this country,
Howling in torment. He may be still alive,
Or he may now be dead. You will soon see.   790
This is the plot I have caught you carrying out
Against my father. May you be punished for it
By Justice the avenger and the Furies!
This is my curse, if it is right to curse you;
And it is right, for you have made it right
By killing the noblest man in all the world,
Whose equal you will never see again.

DEIANEIRA moves away

CHORUS:

    Leaving without a word? Surely you know
    Your silence takes the side of your accuser.

                    Exit DEIANEIRA

HYLLUS:

    Do not prevent her! Let a favoring wind   800
    Blow her, no matter where, out of my sight!
    Why should she bear the honored name of mother
    When what she does is so unlike a mother?
    No. Let her go. Farewell to her. And may
    She find the happiness she gave my father.

                    Exit HYLLUS

CHORUS:

      See, women, see! The prophecy uttered of old
  By the voice of the god is upon us now on a sudden
     That said, when the tale of twelve full years was told,
  The true-born son of Zeus from all the labors
     Which he had been forced to endure would find release, 810
  And surely that word has come home safe to harbor,
  For in the underworld a man no longer
     Is wearied by his toil but is at peace.

      How can he hope to see tomorrow's light,
  Caught in the net of death by the crafty centaur?
     The clinging venom begins to burn and bite,
  Begotten by Death and bred by the gleaming serpent.
     He is pierced with agony from head to feet,
  Tightly held in the coils of the terrible Hydra,
  And the murderous goads blister and spread and rankle 820
     That black-haired Nessus fashioned by his deceit.

  Poor woman, she saw that a second union was bringing
     Disaster on her home, yet all
  That has come to pass because of the stranger's counsel
    At that dread meeting she did not foresee.
  But now in despair she utters her lamentation,
     In teeming showers her soft tears fall;
  And doom makes evident as it approaches
     The ruin born of treachery.

  Our streaming tears break out for that glorious hero. 830
     He is consumed by agony
  Greater than any pain his foes had inflicted.

We weep for the dark head of that mighty spear
That fought in the forefront of battle, that sent this
    maiden
From Oechalia swiftly across the sea.
But this was the work of Cyprian Aphrodite:
Her silent ministry is clear.

A cry off-stage

SEMI-CHORUS 1:
    Was I mistaken, or did I hear just now
    Someone inside there crying out in grief?
SEMI-CHORUS 2:
    There is no doubt it was a shriek of anguish.   840
    Some new affliction is upon this house.

Enter NURSE

CHORUS:
    Look! There is the old woman, frowning, strangely
    Unlike herself, coming to bring us news.
NURSE:
    O women, women! Sorrow has come upon us.
    That gift to Heracles was the beginning.
CHORUS:
    What grief have you to tell of now, old woman?
NURSE:
    Deianeira has not moved a single step
    Yet she has taken the last of all her journeys.
CHORUS:
    You mean that she is dead? NURSE: You have heard my
        news.
CHORUS:
    How pitiful! Dead? NURSE: I say so once again.   850
CH.:   Poor creature! Can you tell us how she perished?
NUR.:   Her deed was harrowing.
CH.:   Speak, woman, speak! What was the fate she met with?
NUR.:   She killed herself.
CH.:   What rage, what frenzy winged the cruel weapon
        That cut her down! One death upon another
        And both her doing! What means did she find for this
            one?
NUR.:   The stroke of a bitter sword.
CH.:   You yourself saw her violent act, old woman?
NUR.:   I saw it. I was there.   860
CH.:   What did she do? How did she do it? Tell us.
NUR.:   She killed herself unaided.
CH.:   What are you saying? NURSE: The truth, pure and simple.
CH.:   That new bride's first-born child is Vengeance.
        Death inherits this household.

65

NURSE:
>It does indeed. If you had seen what happened,
>You would have felt still greater pity for her.

CHORUS:
>How could a woman do what she has done?

NURSE:
>It was heart-rending, as you will agree
>Once you have heard my story. When she came   870
>Into the house alone and saw her son
>Preparing in the court a deep, soft litter
>To take back when he went to meet his father,
>She hid herself from everyone, and falling
>Beside the altars, mourned their desolation.
>And wept, poor creature, when she touched some object
>She had once used; or when she roamed about
>From room to room and saw some slave she loved,
>Her tears burst forth. She cried aloud, bewailing
>Her own fate and the fate of all her household.   880
>At last she stopped, and suddenly I saw her
>Rush into Heracles' room. I watched in hiding
>And saw her spread a covering on his bed.
>And then, when she had finished, she sprang up
>And sat there in the middle. With hot tears
>Falling in streams she cried, "Oh, bridal bed
>And bridal chamber! all is over now.
>Farewell forever, I shall nevermore
>Enjoy your welcome and sleep here in peace.
>Then, with no further words, she wrenched apart   890
>The gold brooch on her breast, loosening her robe,
>Baring her whole left arm and side. I ran
>As fast as I could go to tell her son
>What she intended, but between the time
>I left her and the time that we returned
>We found that she had taken a two-edged sword
>And stabbed it through her side into her heart.
>Her son shrieked at the sight. Poor man, he knew
>She had been driven to do this by his anger,
>And he had learned too late from household servants   900
>That she had followed in all innocence
>The centaur's prompting. Then the wretched boy
>Broke out in passionate lamentation, wailing,
>Kneeling to shower down kisses on her lips,
>Throwing himself beside her on the ground,
>Crying aloud that he had struck her down
>With his wicked accusation, bathed in tears
>Because at one stroke he had been deprived
>Of both his parents. That is what has happened.

Only a rash man counts on anything   910
Beyond today. Tomorrow cannot be,
Until today is safely past and gone.

                            Exit NURSE

CHORUS:
   Which of these is the worse disaster?
     For which shall my first tears flow?
     My heart is too heavy within me
       For me to know.

   There in the house I can see one sorrow.
     The next I await, undone.
     Suffering and expectation —
       The two are one.   920

   Would I might feel a fair wind blowing
   Strong and fresh on this house to bear me
      Far far away
   Out of this land, lest I die of terror
   Only to look at the man, the mighty
     Son of Zeus! He is coming, they say,
   Helpless from torments nothing can allay —
     A sight beyond all telling awful.

   Close at hand is the grief I foreboded,
   Crying aloud like a nightingale, shrilly.   930
      Look! It is here.
   Yonder they come, not men of our country,
   Slowly, with measured pace, in silence.
     Like those who are tending someone dear
   They bear him with them; they are drawing near.
     What does it mean? Is he dead or sleeping?

        Enter HYLLUS *and* OLD MAN
       HERACLES *is carried in on a litter*

HYLLUS:
   Oh, father, father!
   Oh how I grieve for you!
   What can I do? I am lost, lost without you!

OLD MAN:
   Hush, my boy, hush. Do not rouse the pain   940
   That drives him to fury. He is alive,
   Barely alive. Restrain yourself.

HYLLUS:
   What did you say? Is he living?

OLD MAN:
   He is asleep. You must not wake him

Or you will bring to life again
His intermittent agony.

HYLLUS:

This burden of grief is crushing.
I am going mad in my sorrow.

HERACLES:

Oh Zeus! Where am I?
Who are these people beside me?   950
Here where I lie in endless torment?
Oh! What agony! Once more
This horrible stuff is devouring me!

OLD MAN:

You see? You should have kept your grief
From breaking out instead of driving
Sleep from his brain and eyes.

HYLLUS:

No, no! I cannot be patient
Seeing such misery.

HERACLES:

A cruel repayment, O Zeus,
For the splendid sacrifice I offered   960
On the altar stones of Cenaeum!
I am given over to ruin, to utter ruin.
Would I had never laid eyes on the place
That brought this frenzy upon me,
The piercing spasms of this unquenchable pain.
What weaver of spells, save only Zeus,
What healer, what skilled physician
Can soothe, can assuage my anguish? Even to catch
A distant glimpse of him would be a marvel.
Leave me, leave me here in my suffering.   970
Let me sleep my last sleep.
Why do you touch me? Why do you move me?
Oh! You are killing me, killing me!
You have wakened my torment — if it ever slept.
Again! Oh! Oh! This foul thing fastens upon me.
Where are you, most thankless of Greeks? I wore myself
                           out for you,
Ridding your seas and thickets of monsters.
Now *I* am stricken. Will no one show me
The mercy of fire or a sword?
Will no one, no one come who is willing   980
To strike off the head from my loathsome body?

OLD MAN (*bending over* HERACLES):

This is beyond my strength. Here, help me.
You are his son and can do more
Than I to give him some relief.

HYLLUS:

    I have him in my arms, but I can never
    Make him forget his torments, nor can anyone.
    Zeus has ordained them.

HERACLES:

    Son, son! Where are you? Help me. Take hold of me.
    There. Lift me up. What a fate I suffer!
    Once more this appalling pollution   990
    Clutches me, tears me to pieces
    In its irresistible fury.
    O Pallas, Pallas! It renews its torture!
    Be merciful, son, to your father.
    Draw out your sword — you could never be blamed for
            it —
    Stab me here in my breast. Put an end
    To this maddening pain that your godless mother in-
        flicted.
    Oh, to see her struck down as she struck me down,
    Dying my death! Kind Hades,
    Brother of Zeus, give me sleep, give me sleep.   1000
    Cut short this agony by some swift doom.

CHORUS:

    I shudder, friends, to hear lord Heracles' pain,
    So great a man, suffering so cruelly.

HERACLES:

    Deed after fearful deed these hands have done,
    Load after heavy load this back has borne,
    Grievous even to tell of. Yet no labor
    Exacted from me by the wife of Zeus
    Or loathed Eurystheus could approach this torment,
    Which that deceitful woman, Oeneus' daughter,
    Wrapped round my shoulders, the Furies' woven net   1010
    In which I perish. Glued against my sides,
    It has gnawed through me to my very vitals,
    Living within me, cutting off my breath.
    My fresh blood it has drained away already.
    From head to foot my body is corrupted,
    Held in the grip of these unspeakable fetters.
    Neither the foemen's spears on the field of battle,
    Nor the host of earth-born giants, nor the might
    Of savage beasts could ever accomplish this,
    Nor any land that I have purified,   1020
    Greek or barbarian. Yet a weak woman,
    Without man's inborn powers, alone, unarmed,
    Has brought me low. My son, now show yourself
    In truth my son. Do not give greater honor
    To a mother's name. Bring her out here yourself,

That woman who bore you. Turn her over to me.
Then I will know which sight will hurt you more,
My torture or the torture she will suffer,
Which she deserves so greatly. Go, son, go.
Be brave enough for this, have pity on me,   1030
For to most men I would seem pitiful,
Moaning and weeping like a girl — a thing
No one could say he had seen me do till now.
Without a murmur I have always gone
Where my ill fortune led me. Now, poor wretch,
I am found to be a woman. Come. Stand here
At your father's side, and see the calamity
I have endured. There! I will lift the covers.
All of you look at this poor, agonized body.
Look at this misery, this wretchedness.   1040
Oh, horrible!
Once more, once more these spasms of pain convulse me.
They are piercing me through and through like bursts
                    of flame.
This cruel, consuming poison gives me no peace,
Lord Hades, take me!
Smite me, lightning of Zeus!
Hurl down your thunderbolt, lord Zeus, upon me.
Launch it against me, father, for this venom
Begins again to devour me. It has burst
Into full flower. It has broken loose.   1050
O hands, O back and breast and trusty arms!
It was you, you whose strength in bygone days
Subdued that savage and intractable creature,
That scourge of herdsmen, the Nemean lion:
Subdued the Lernean Hydra, and that host
Of barbarous monsters, man and horse combined,
Insolent, lawless, of surpassing strength;
The Erymánthian boar; and underground
That triple-headed beast, the hound of Hades,
Invincible offspring of the dread Echídna;   1060
And in the farthest reaches of the earth
The guardian dragon of the golden apples.
I have had countless hardships, but these hands
Never gave up the prize of victory.
Now with my strength gone and my body mangled
I am the prey of an unseen destroyer —
I, who am called the son of a noble mother,
I, who am called the son of Zeus, the lord
Of the starry heavens. Yet I tell you this,
Though I am nothing, nothing that even crawls,   1070
Even so these hands will crush her. Let her only

Come here to me. Then she can give my message
To the whole world: I punished evil-doers
All of my life, and punished them as I died.

CHORUS:

Unhappy Greece! I can foresee great sorrow
In store for you, if you must lose this man.

HYLLUS:

Let me speak, father, now that you are silent,
However great your suffering may be.
I wish to ask only for what is right.
Listen to what I tell you, quietly,   1080
Without this storm of anger. Otherwise
You cannot learn that the revenge you long for
Is out of reach and that your rage is groundless.

HERACLES:

Say what you want and get it over with.
I am in too much pain to solve your riddles.

HYLLUS:

I have come to tell you how my mother is,
And that the wrong she did was unintended.

HERACLES:

You utter scoundrel! To let me hear you mention
Your mother's name, when she has killed your father.

HYLLUS:

As she is now, silence would not be right.   1090

HERACLES:

No, it would not, considering her past crimes.

HYLLUS:

And today's happenings, as you will admit.

HERACLES:

Take care not to disgrace yourself, but speak.

HYLLUS:

I will. She is dead. She has been killed just now.

HERACLES:

What! Who has killed her? How I hate to hear it!

HYLLUS:

No one else did it. She has killed herself.

HERACLES:

I cannot bear the thought. I should have killed her.

HYLLUS:

If you knew the truth, even you could not be angry.

HERACLES:

A strange way to begin. What do you mean?

HYLLUS:

The fact is she did wrong but she meant well.   1100

71

HERACLES:
>Villain! She meant well when she killed your father?

HYLLUS:
>With that new bride inside the house, she meant
>To apply a love charm, but her plan miscarried.

HERACLES:
>Who here in Trachis deals with drugs like that?

HYLLUS:
>Nessus, the centaur, long ago induced her
>To kindle your desire with such a charm.

HERACLES:
>Oh! Oh! I am lost! Lost! Wretch that I am!
>The light of day will shine for me no longer.
>I know now the calamity that has happened.
>Go, son. Your father's end has come. Go call   1110
>Your brothers, all of them, and call Alcmena —
>She was the bride of Zeus in vain, poor woman —
>To hear the oracles that concern my death.

HYLLUS:
>Your mother, as it happens, is away.
>She is on the coast at Tiryns and has taken
>Some of the children there to live with her;
>And others, I can tell you, are at Thebes.
>We who are here will do our utmost, father,
>To be of any service that is needed.

HERACLES:
>Then listen, and do your duty. Now is the time   1120
>For you to show what kind of man you are,
>You who are called my son. Long since, my father
>Revealed to me that I should not be killed
>By any living creature, but by one
>Who had gone to dwell in Hades. Now I am slain
>By the savage centaur, the living by the dead,
>And the divine prediction is fulfilled.
>And I will show how later prophecies
>Agree with this and give it their support.
>In the Selli's grove — the mountain folk who sleep   1130
>Upon the ground — I wrote these sayings down
>As they were given me by my father's oak,
>The oak of many voices. I was told
>That when this moment that is now upon me
>Came into being, I should be released
>From all the toils with which I had been burdened.
>And I supposed that meant I would be happy,
>But it meant only that I was to die,
>Because the dead have rest. Beyond all doubt
>These prophecies have proved true. So then, my son,   1140
>You must be ready once again to help me.

Do not delay until I goad you on.
Take my part freely. Find out for yourself
The best of laws — obedience to a father.

HYLLUS:
I am afraid of what your words must mean,
But I will do whatever you wish me to.

HERACLES:
Then first of all, put your right hand in mine.

HYLLUS:
But why do you insist on such a promise?

HERACLES:
Your hand. At once. No disobedience.

HYLLUS:
Look. There it is. I will refuse you nothing.   1150

HERACLES:
Swear by my father, by the head of Zeus.

HYLLUS:
What must I swear to? I will promise it.

HERACLES:
You must perform the duty that I give you.

HYLLUS:
I swear. Let Zeus be witness to my oath.

HERACLES:
And pray that if you break it you may suffer.

HYLLUS:
I do. But I am true. I shall not suffer.

HERACLES:
Well then, you know Mt. Oeta, Zeus's peak?

HYLLUS:
Yes. On those heights I have often sacrificed.

HERACLES:
Carry me there yourself, with your own hands,
Getting what friends you want to help you; cut   1160
And heap up boughs of firmly rooted oak
And tough wild olive; lay my body on them,
And with a flaming pine torch kindle it.
There must be no display of grief, no tears,
No lamentation, if you are a son of mine.
But if you disobey, my curse shall reach you,
Even from Hades, and forever crush you.

HYLLUS:
Father! What are you telling me to do?

HERACLES:
What you will have to do. If you refuse,
Call yourself son of someone else, not me.   1170

HYLLUS:
How can I bear it, father! You would make me
Your murderer, polluted with your blood.

HERACLES:

> No, not at all. I make you my physician,
> The only man to heal my suffering.

HYLLUS:

> How can I heal your body when I burn it?

HERACLES:

> If that dismays you, do the rest at least.

HYLLUS:

> I will take you there. I could not grudge you that.

HERACLES:

> And you will build the pyre as I directed?

HYLLUS:

> I cannot put my hands on it myself.
> I will do everything else, you may be sure.   1180

HERACLES:

> Well, that will be enough. And now, my son,
> Having done so much, do one small service more.

HYLLUS:

> Yes, certainly, however great it is.

HERACLES:

> Eurytus had a daughter. Do you know her?

HYLLUS:

> I suppose the girl you mean is Iolé.

HERACLES:

> She is the one, and this is my command.
> When I am dead, if you intend to show
> Your piety and keep the oath you swore,
> Then do not disboey, but marry her.
> No other man can be allowed to have her   1190
> Since I have lain with her. You are the one
> Who must become her husband. Do what I tell you.
> You have been loyal in important matters,
> But if you prove disloyal in this small one,
> You cancel all my debt of gratitude.

HYLLUS:

> You are in pain. I ought not to be angry,
> But that idea is unendurable.

HERACLES:

> That does not sound as though you would obey me.

HYLLUS:

> Who could? When she, she only, drove my mother
> To kill herself, and made you what you are?   1200
> No one could do that of his own free will
> Unless he was driven mad by the gods of vengeance.
> Father, I would be better dead myself
> Than married to my bitterest enemy.

74

HERACLES:

> The man will not defer to me, it seems,
> Though I am dying. But if you ignore
> What I command, the curse of the gods awaits you.

HYLLUS:

> Soon you will show, I am sure, how sick you are.

HERACLES:

> Yes, for you rouse my agony from its sleep.

HYLLUS:

> Awful! Where shall I turn? I am bewildered.   1210

HERACLES:

> Because you choose to disregard my words.

HYLLUS:

> But am I now to learn impiety?

HERACLES:

> To warm my heart is no impiety.

HYLLUS:

> You order me? You justify the act?

HERACLES:

> I do, and call the gods as witnesses.

HYLLUS:

> Then I will not refuse, but may the gods
> Hear me: you are responsible for this.
> I cannot be condemned if I obey you.

HERACLES:

> At last you have spoken well. Now lose no time
> In making good your promise. Lay me on the pyre   1220
> Before the pain returns to sting and rend me.
> Come. Quickly. Lift me up. This is true rest
> From all my troubles. This is my ultimate end.

HYLLUS:

> Nothing prevents that consummation, father,
> Since you command us and we have no choice.

HERACLES:

> O my hardened soul, while the pain is sleeping,
> Set my lips like stone together;
> Curb them with steel lest a cry escape them,
> Since the harsh fate that lies before me
> Will prove most welcome.   1230

HYLLUS:

> You who follow him, lift him up.
> For what I do grant me forgiveness,
> And mark the gods' great cruelty
> When such things happen. They have fathered
> Children by whom they are invoked,
> And gaze untroubled on their torment.
> No one knows what the future brings,

75

But the present for us is a time of sorrow,
For the gods above, a time of shame,
And a time of anguish beyond example   1240
For him who endures this doom.

CHORUS:
And women, you too come. Make no excuse
For staying in this house. Here you beheld
A dreadful death, tortures unparalleled.
And everything that you beheld is Zeus.

Electra

CHARACTERS IN THE PLAY

ELECTRA, *daughter of* CLYTEMNESTRA *and* AGAMEMNON

CHRYSOTHEMIS, *daughter of* CLYTEMNESTRA *and* AGAMEMNON

ORESTES, *son of* CLYTEMNESTRA *and* AGAMEMNON

CLYTEMNESTRA, *wife of* AEGISTHUS

AEGISTHUS, *King of Mycenae*

PYLADES, *friend of* ORESTES

OLD MAN, *retainer and companion of* ORESTES

CHORUS *of Mycenaean women*

ELECTRA

SCENE: *Mycenae. Before the palace of* AGAMEMNON

Enter OLD MAN, ORESTES, *and* PYLADES

OLD MAN:

Son of King Agamemnon, son of him
Who led our armies years ago at Troy,
Now you may see what you have always longed for.
There is your heart's desire, time-honored Argos,
The sacred spot from which the gad-fly drove
The child of Inachus. Look there, Orestes!
The forum of the god, wolf-slaying Lycius,
And on the left the famous temple of Hera.
Mycenae lies before us, rich in gold.
There is the house of Pelops and his race,   10
The house made desolate by so much bloodshed.
I took you from your sister, when your father
Was murdered there, brought you away in safety,
And cared for you till you had grown to manhood
To be the avenger of your father's death.
Orestes, and you, Pýladés, the friend
He holds most dear, we must take counsel quickly.
See! It is dawning, and the sun's bright rays
Waken the birds, whose songs are ringing clear.
The darkness of the starry night is gone.   20
We must be ready before anyone
Comes from the palace, for we do not dare
Hesitate now. The time is ripe for action.

ORESTES:

How true a friend and follower of my house
You show yourself in this! You urge us on
And follow closely, like a thoroughbred horse,
Who pricks his ears up in the face of danger,
Still full of courage in spite of being old.
And so I will tell you what I have decided.
Pay close attention, and if anything   30
I say is wrong, correct me. When I went
To the oracle at Delphi to discover
How to avenge the murder of my father,
Phoebus Apollo gave me this response:
I was to gain my just revenge by stealth,
Through my own stratagem, unseconded
By an armed force. That was the oracle,
And therefore when you see your chance to enter

79

The house there, go, and find out everything
That they are doing, so that you may give us   40
A clear report of it. They will not know you,
For how could they suspect? Long years have passed,
You have grown old, your hair is streaked with white.
Say that you are a stranger, who has come
From Phocis, and that Phánoteus has sent you —
Of all their allies, he is the most important.
Tell them, and swear an oath that you speak truly,
Orestes met his fate by being flung
From his swift chariot at the Pythian games.
Let that, in substance, be your story. Meanwhile   50
We first will honor, as the god commanded,
My father's tomb by pouring out libations
And strewing locks of hair; and then come back
With the bronze urn that, as you know, is hidden
There in the woods. By this we will confirm
The false report they will be glad to hear
That my dead body has been burned to ashes.
Why should the rumor of my death disturb me
When I in fact win safety and renown?
To me, no story is an evil omen   60
That turns to my advantage. I have heard
Of many clever men who have been falsely
Reported dead, and have come home again
To even greater honors than before.
So I exult in thinking that I too
On my appearance shall disperse these rumors
And blaze out like a star upon my foes.
Hear me, my country and my country's gods!
May all go well with me in my return.
Halls of my fathers! Since the gods have sent me   70
To purge you of corruption, grant I may not
Leave in disgrace, but rather that I may
Regain my heritage and restore my house.
But I have spoken long enough. Old friend,
Go do your part, and we two will do ours,
For opportunity is beckoning us,
And the right moment rules the affairs of men.

ELECTRA (*within*):
  Ah, miserable!

OLD MAN:
  Did you hear that? Someone, I thought, was crying,
  Some slave girl there inside the palace door.   80

ORESTES:
  Can it have been the sad voice of Electra?
  Shall we stay here and listen to her grief?

OLD MAN:

 No. Our first task is to obey Apollo.
To pour out our libations to your father
Will prove a good beginning that will give us
The advantage now and victory in the end.

     Exeunt ORESTES, OLD MAN, *and* PYLADES
      Enter ELECTRA *from the house*

ELECTRA:

 O most pure light!
O realm of air wide as the earth beneath you!
How often have you heard my loud lamenting,
 How often, as the night   90
Yielded at last to morning, have you seen me
Raining wild blows upon my blood-stained bosom.
 And you, my hated bed, know well
How in that dismal house I keep my vigil,
 Mourning my father. Not in some distant country
Did death come to him as the gift of Ares;
 But at my mother's hands he fell.
My mother and her bedfellow Aegísthus
 Brought down upon his head the death I weep;
For like a woodman's axe that fells an oak tree 100
 Their murderous axe struck deep.
Father, your fate was pitiful and cruel,
 And I, I only, mourn you.

  But never will I have done
With pouring out the great flood of my sorrow,
While I yet see the glitter of the starlight
 Or the bright sun.
 But as the nightingale,
The slayer of her child, forevermore
 Gives utterance to her pain, so I too wail,   110
So I too cry aloud, cry without ceasing
 Here at my father's door.
O home of Hades and Perséphoné!
 O awful Curse! O guide of shades, lord Hermes!
O Furies, fearful daughters of the immortals!
 You who see
A man struck down, a marriage-bed dishonored,
 Give me your aid, grant me my plea!
Avenge my father's murder, let my brother
 Return to me. My crushing grief has grown 120
Too heavy a load for me to bear alone.

       Enter CHORUS

CHORUS:

> Ah, poor Electra, child of a wicked mother!
> Why are the tears unending that you shed
> For Agamemnon? He has long been dead,
> Entangled in your mother's treacherous snare.
> The deed was shameful. May the doer perish,
> If I may be permitted such a prayer.

EL.:

> You have come to soothe me, my friends, to give me
>   comfort.
> You are constant, generous, kind: all this I know.
> And yet I cannot change; for my poor father   130
>   My tears forever flow,
> For him my lamentation never ends.
> Your hearts are always loving and responsive.
>   Leave me I beg you, friends,
>   In my distraction.

CHORUS:

> But no laments, no prayers can bring your father
>   Back to the living from the world below,
>   From that dark water to which all must go.
> Immoderate sorrow leaves you without relief,
>   Hopeless and helpless before life-long evil.   140
> Why are you still abandoned to your grief?

EL.:

> What folly for a child not to remember
>   A parent's piteous death! More dear to me
> Is that bird, pierced with sorrow, Zeus's herald,
>   Who everlastingly
> For Itys, Itys makes her stricken moan.
> Ah, Níobé! I worship you, in anguish,
>   Shut in your tomb of stone,
>   Weeping forever.

CHORUS:

> But no calamity has come upon you   150
>   That only you, Electra, have to bear.
> This desperate grief of yours is for an evil
>   That your two sisters, living with you, share.
> And young Orestes grieves in his seclusion.
>   Yet happiness awaits him, for the hand
> Of kindly Zeus shall lead him, and Mycenae
>   Shall welcome him as lord of this great land.

EL.:

>   For long years I have yearned
> To have him here, living in expectation,
> Unwedded, childless, doomed to unceasing sorrow.   160
>   Yet he forgets, forgets what he has learned,
>   What he has suffered, for to every word
> That he has sent me he has proved unfaithful

82

He longs to return, and yet for all his longing
  He has not stirred.

CHORUS:
  Take courage, child. Commit your violent anger
   To Zeus all-seeing, who in heaven reigns,
  And yield not utterly to thoughts of vengeance.
   Time is a god assuaging mortal pains.
  By Crisa's shore, the pasture land of oxen,   170
   King Agamemnon's son is living yet.
  He is not heedless, he has not forgotten,
   Nor does the god of Acheron forget.

EL.:   Hopeless and in despair
  I waste away. Most of my life is over,
  And all my strength is gone. I have no children,
   No man to shield me with his loving care.
   But like an alien, a detested thing,
  I do my household tasks, with rags to clothe me,
  And eat my scraps of food here where my father 180
   Was once the king.

CHORUS:
  Pitiful was the cry at his returning
  And at his feast, when the bronze axe fell swiftly
   In one sure-handed blow.
  Trickery wove the plot, lust was the slayer,
  Awful begetters of an awful outcome,
   Whether a god or mortal laid him low.

EL.: O bitter day, bitter beyond compare,
  When I was taken captive! O unspeakable banquet!
   The night my father saw that treacherous pair 190
    Strike without pity!
  O Zeus, take vengeance! Let them suffer all
  The agonies they have made others suffer.
   Let them find no joy in their triumph. To thee I call,
    Thou mighty lord of Olympus.

CHORUS:
  Be well advised, Electra. Speak no further.
  You have heaped up needless woe by your behavior.
   Cannot you understand?
  Your bitter soul is still engaged in warfare.
  You must not let this grow to open conflict 200
   Against the strong when they are in command.

EL.: So terrible a deed gave me no choice.
  I know, I know the violence of my passion,
   But till I perish it will find a voice
    In my wild outcries.
   You have loving hearts, friends, but no words can cure

Such injuries as mine. Console me no longer.
I can find no relief from the sorrows I now endure.
I can never silence my wailing.

CHORUS:

At least with a mother's tenderness I urge you   210
Not to bring endless woes upon your head.

EL.:   But how can they ever end? Is it a virtue
To disregard the dead?
Is that belief inborn? I want no praise
From him who has it. And in future days
If I should reach some tranquil haven,
Let me not be content
With selfish ease there; let me not shame my father
By folding shut the wings of my lament.
For if henceforth he is to be as nothing,   220
Dead in the dust,
His killers alive, his murder unrequited,
Then will all reverence for the gods, all trust
In human justice disappear forever.

CHORUS:

I came for your sake, child, as well as mine,
And yet if you dislike what I have said,
Do as you wish, and we will follow you.

ELECTRA:

I am ashamed, my friends, to have you think me
Too passionate in such constant lamentations,
But since I am driven by necessity,   230
Be patient with me. How could any woman
Who is well-born, how could she hold her peace,
If she had seen, as I see day and night,
Her father's house polluted, with the stain
Not fading out but growing ever deeper?
And as for me, the mother who gave me birth
Has come to be my bitter enemy.
My father's murderers live in my home,
Theirs is the rule, they give me or refuse me
The necessities of life. And think, friends, think   240
Of how I pass my days, seeing Aegisthus
Seated upon my royal father's throne,
Wearing my father's robes, and pouring out
Libations on the hearth at which he killed him;
And as the ultimate outrage, seeing him,
That murderer, lying in my father's bed
Beside my mother, if his bedfellow
Deserves that name. She is so lost to shame
That, steeped though he is in blood, she lives with him
And does not fear the Furies. No, exulting,   250

In bitter mockery, she marks the day
On which she treacherously killed my father
By monthly celebrations: dance, and song,
And sacrifices to the gods that saved her.
But I — how miserable! — I see all this,
And in the palace there, grieve and lament,
Wailing the wicked feast named for my father,
Wasting away with the tears I shed in secret,
Since I am not allowed to weep my fill.
For she, so noble in her protestations,   260
Takes me to task with loud and bitter words:
"You godless, hateful girl! Does no one else
Weep for a father? No one mourn some loss?
I curse you, and I pray the gods below
Never to dry your tears." So she insults me;
But when she is told Orestes is returning,
Then she comes storming up to me and cries,
"You are responsible! This is your doing!
You stole Orestes from me and saw to it
That he escaped. You can be very sure   270
That you will get the punishment you deserve."
And as she shrieks at me, her famous husband
Urges her on and echoes her — that weakling,
That utter scoundrel, who fights all his battles
With women's help. But I am sick at heart,
Waiting, eternally waiting for Orestes
To come and end these miseries. He has been
Always about to act, but any hope
That I could once have had has been destroyed.
How can I, then, be self-controlled, my friends,   280
Or reverent? When I am wronged so deeply,
I have no choice but to retaliate.

CHORUS:
　　Now tell me. Has Aegisthus been at home
　　While you were speaking, or has he gone away?

ELECTRA:
　　You may be sure I would not have come outside
　　Had he been home. No. He is in the country.

CHORUS:
　　If that is so, then may I speak more freely?

ELECTRA:
　　He is not here. What do you want to ask?

CHORUS:
　　This: what have you to tell us of your brother?
　　Will he come soon, or will he still delay?   290

ELECTRA:
　　He promises to come, and breaks his word.

8 5

CHORUS:
> With some great deed to do, a man will pause.

ELECTRA:
> I never paused. Not when I rescued *him*.

CHORUS:
> Take courage. He is noble and will help us.

ELECTRA:
> I would be dead without that hope to cling to.

CHORUS:
> Say no more now. There at the door I see
> Chrysóthemis, your sister, born of the same
> Parents as you, and in her hands she brings
> The gifts men offer to the dead below.
>
> *Enter* CHRYSOTHEMIS

CHRYSOTHEMIS:
> Sister! Why have you come outdoors again?   300
> Why do you make another scene in public?
> After so many years you should have learned
> Not to indulge yourself in useless anger.
> Truly, I too am grieved at what has happened
> To both of us. If I were strong enough,
> I would soon show them how I felt about them,
> But in a storm like this to shorten sail
> Seems best to me. I have no power to act,
> And empty threats are foolish. How I wish
> You would follow my example! It is true   310
> That what you chose, and not what I advise,
> Is the right course, and yet to live in freedom
> I must obey our rulers without question.

ELECTRA:
> How strange it is that you, with such a father,
> Should disregard him and should heed your mother.
> She taught you all these warnings that you give me.
> Not one word is your own. Now take your choice:
> Either act rashly, or in prudent wisdom
> Forget those close to you. You have just said
> If you could find strength, you would show your hatred;   320
> Yet when I do my best to avenge my father,
> You give no help, and even try to stop me.
> Is not this cowardice on top of all
> Our woes? Tell me, or listen rather. What
> Have I to gain by stopping these laments?
> Am I not living? Miserably, I know,
> But well enough. And I displease those two
> When to the dead I offer up my tribute,
> Provided gratitude exists in Hades.
> You say you hate them. Do your actions show it?   330

You live in friendship with the murderers.
But I would not submit, though I were given
Those gifts of theirs on which you pride yourself:
A lavish table, a luxurious life.
To do no violence to my convictions
Is food enough for me. I do not want
The privilege you have, nor would you either,
If you were wise. Men might have called you child
Of the most noble father in the world.
Let them now call you daughter of your mother!   340
Thus everyone will know how vile you are,
Betraying your dead father and your kindred.

CHORUS:
I beg you not to quarrel. Each of you
Has spoken well, and each of you could profit
From what was said, if you would learn to listen.

CHRYSOTHEMIS:
My friends, her tirades are not new to me.
I would never have said a word, had I not learned
That she is threatened with an awful fate
Which will cut short her endless lamentations.

ELECTRA:
Tell me this terror! If it is anything worse   350
Than what I bear now, I will say no more.

CHRYSOTHEMIS:
Then I will tell you everything I know.
If your laments continue, they propose
To send you into exile, to a place
Where you will live shut from the light of day,
And in a dungeon chant your harsh refrain.
Take time to think. Be wise now while you can,
And do not blame me after you have suffered.

ELECTRA:
Is that what they intend to do to me?

CHRYSOTHEMIS:
Yes, certainly. When Aegisthus has come home.   360

ELECTRA:
Let him come quickly then! Let him come quickly!

CHRYSOTHEMIS:
How wrong, how foolish! Why do you say that?

ELECTRA:
I want him here, if those are his intentions.

CHRYSOTHEMIS:
That you may suffer what? Have you gone mad?

ELECTRA:
I will get free from all of you, completely.

CHRYSOTHEMIS:
But does your present life mean nothing to you?

ELECTRA:
Ah yes, my present life. How fine it is!
CHRYSOTHEMIS:
It would be fine, if you controlled yourself.
ELECTRA:
Do not teach me to be false to those I love.
CHRYSOTHEMIS:
No. Only to submit to those in power.   370
ELECTRA:
Not I. I leave such flattery to you.
CHRYSOTHEMIS:
It is good to escape the ruin that comes from folly.
ELECTRA:
To avenge my father I will die if need be.
CHRYSOTHEMIS:
But I know our father pardons me for this.
ELECTRA:
Cowards think highly of that kind of saying.
CHRYSOTHEMIS:
Then you refuse to listen or be persuaded?
ELECTRA:
I will never listen, never be so foolish.
CHRYSOTHEMIS:
In that case I will go about my business.
ELECTRA:
Where are you going? For whom are these offerings meant?
CHRYSOTHEMIS:
Our mother sends them to our father's grave.   380
ELECTRA:
Our mother! To her bitterest enemy?
CHRYSOTHEMIS:
"The man she murdered" you would like to say.
ELECTRA:
What friend persuaded her? Who wanted this?
CHRYSOTHEMIS:
I think that she has had a fearful dream.
ELECTRA:
Gods of our forefathers! Help me now at last!
CHRYSOTHEMIS:
Are you encouraged by her being frightened?
ELECTRA:
I could answer if you told me what she saw.
CHRYSOTHEMIS:
I can say very little of what happened.
ELECTRA:
Still, tell me what you can, for many times
Only a word has wrecked or made men's fortunes.   390

88

CHRYSOTHEMIS:
> I heard this much. She saw our father standing
> Beside her, in the light of day again.
> Then he took up the scepter of Aegisthus,
> That once had been his own, and planted it
> Next to the hearth. From it a fruitful branch
> Budded and spread until it overshadowed
> All of Mycenae. This was what I heard
> From someone who was with her when she told
> Her dream to the Sun God. I know nothing more
> Except that her terror made her send me here.   400
> Listen, Electra! I beg you, by the gods
> That guard our house, not to destroy yourself
> By your own folly. If you reject me now,
> Later in sorrow you will seek my help.

ELECTRA:
> Dear sister, do not let the things you carry
> Come near the tomb. It would be shameful, impious
> To pour libations, or to bring our father
> Gifts that a wife has sent him in her hatred.
> Scatter them to the winds! Bury them deep,
> Where they will never touch our father's grave!   410
> But let them be a treasure laid aside
> In Hades for her when she comes to die.
> She is more shameless than any woman alive,
> Or she would never have wanted you to pour
> A foe's libations to the man she killed.
> Do you suppose that, lying in his grave,
> He would be apt to welcome gifts from one
> Who slew him like an enemy without mercy,
> Mangled him, and to cleanse herself, wiped off
> The bloodstains on his head? Can you believe   420
> That she will be absolved by what you bring?
> It is impossible. Throw those things away,
> And offer him instead a lock of hair
> From your own head; and give on my behalf —
> Poor gifts, but all my wretchedness affords —
> This unanointed hair, this simple girdle.
> Then pray that he may come to us in pity
> From the underworld to help us in our struggle.
> Pray that Orestes, in victorious strength,
> May live to tread his enemies underfoot;   430
> And that in days to come we may be able
> To honor our father's tomb with gifts more splendid
> Than we can give it now. Truly I think
> He helped to send these menacing dreams to her;
> Still, do all this — for me, and for yourself,

And for our father, now at rest in Hades,
The dearest to us of all mortal men.

CHORUS:
Your sister, child, has spoken reverently.
You would be wise to follow her advice.

CHRYSOTHEMIS:
I will. It would be foolishness to quarrel,   440
When we two should be doing our clear duty.
Only, I beg this much of you my friends:
When I begin this task, then do your part
By keeping silence, for if my mother learns
What I have done, I shall pay dearly for it.

Exit CHRYSOTHEMIS

CHORUS:
Unless my wisdom fails, unless I prophesy falsely,
Justice will come, my child, and her coming will not be long.
Before her she sends her omens that show her closely pursuing,
Righteous, triumphantly strong.
Breathing its comfort, filling my heart with courage,   450
The news of this vision came.
Your father, lord of the Hellenes, has not forgotten,
Nor has the axe forgotten the blow that killed him
With outrage and shame.

Roused from their fearful ambush, the brazen-footed Furies
Will come with an army's menace, an army's mighty tread;
For eager lust urged on that pair to a guilty union,
A cursed and forbidden bed.
Therefore I know that this portent marks their ruin,
The partners of this crime.   460
No dream, no oracle can show the future,
If this night's vision fails to fulfill its promise
In its due time.

What ruin has followed that chariot-race of Pelops!
For since that distant and calamitous day
When Mýrtilus was hurled to his destruction
Into the sea, dragged from his golden chariot,
Disaster and affliction have held sway
Over this household.

Enter CLYTEMNESTRA

CLYTEMNESTRA:
So then, you seem to wander where you please   470
Now that Aegisthus is not here. He always
Kept you indoors to save your friends from shame;
But in his absence you show me no respect,
In spite of having called me time after time

In public an unjust, presumptuous tyrant,
Malicious in my treatment of you. No,
I am not insolent, I only speak
As I have often heard you speak to me,
Insult for insult. Your eternal pretext
Is that I killed your father. Yes, I killed him. 480
Of course I did. I never would deny it,
For justice struck him down, not I alone.
And if you had your senses, you would do well
To support the cause of justice, since that father,
Whom you are always mourning, was the only
Man among all the Hellenes who could bear
To sacrifice your sister to the gods —
He who as father felt no pain of childbirth.
Tell me! Why did he sacrifice his daughter?
For whose sake did he do it? For the Argives? 490
They had no right to kill her. For his brother,
For Menelaus? If, to spare *him*, he killed her,
Was he not forced to give *me* satisfaction?
His brother had two children. Should not they
Have died before my daughter, since they were born
To parents for whose sake that fleet set sail?
Did Hades long to feast upon my child
Rather than hers? Or was that infamous father
Fond of his brother's children, when he no longer
Felt any love for mine? He was a callous, 500
Unnatural parent. That I am certain of,
Although you disagree; and your dead sister,
If she could speak, would say what I have said.
Therefore the past can hold no terrors for me,
But if you think me wicked, first be sure
You are clear-sighted when you sit in judgment.

ELECTRA:

This time you cannot say my bitterness
Provoked you to an outburst such as that.
But let me do one thing: let me make clear
The truth about my father and my sister. 510

CLYTEMNESTRA:

Yes, you may do it. If you always took
This attitude, I would not hate to hear you.

ELECTRA:

Then I will speak. You say you killed my father.
What could you say more utterly disgraceful?
Justice can make no difference. But I tell you
Justice was not your motive. You were induced
To kill him by that scoundrel whom you married.
Ask Artemis, the huntress, what offense
She punished when she held the winds in check

At Aulis — or I will tell, since it is wrong 520
To question her. My father, it is said,
Going for pastime to her sacred wood,
Once shot and killed a dappled, antlered stag
His footfalls had disturbed, and afterward
Made some chance boast about it. This so angered
The goddess that she made the Greeks her captives
Until my father offered life for life,
His own child for the deer. Her death alone
Allowed the ships to sail for home or Troy.
For their sake, then, and not for Menelaus, 530
At last, against his will, he was compelled
To kill her. But even granting what you said,
Granting he did it for his brother's sake,
Why should you kill him? What law sanctions you?
Beware of making such a law for others;
You may regret it bitterly for yourself.
For if we are to kill to avenge a killing,
Then you, in justice, should be first to die.
The excuse you make is no excuse at all;
For tell me, if you will, why you are living 540
A life of the utmost shame, the bedfellow
Of your accomplice in my father's murder,
Bearing him children, stained as he is with blood,
While you cast off your older, lawful children
Born of a lawful marriage. Can I praise
Actions like these? Or are you going to say
That they too are your vengeance for your daughter?
A vile excuse to make! It is indecent
To wed an enemy for a daughter's sake.
But how can I even advise you, when you shriek 550
That I revile my mother? Yet you seem
Less of a mother to me than a tyrant
So wretched is my life, so full of evils
That you inflict on me — you and your partner.
Your other child, long-suffering Orestes,
Who barely escaped you, languishes in exile.
Time and again I have heard your accusation
That I have brought him up to be an avenger.
You can be certain that I would have done so
Had I been able. So then, if you choose to, 560
Tell the whole world about me, say that I
Am loud-mouthed, or impertinent, or wicked.
If these are my accomplishments, I am
A daughter almost worthy of her mother.

CHORUS:

I see that she is angry and no longer
Gives any thought to the justice of her words.

CLYTEMNESTRA:
> And why should I give any thought to her,
> A full-grown woman who insults her mother?
> Do you suppose that she will feel ashamed
> Of anything, no matter what she does?   570

ELECTRA:
> You will not listen when I tell you truly
> I *am* ashamed. I know that my behavior
> Is unbecoming, that it disgraces me;
> But your hostility, your persecution
> Force me to do such things against my will.
> Degrading conduct teaches degradation.

CLYTEMNESTRA:
> How impudent you are! Talking and talking
> About what I have said, what I have done!

ELECTRA:
> The talk is yours, not mine. You do the deeds,
> And deeds like yours find words that will express them.   580

CLYTEMNESTRA:
> Now by our lady Artemis! Aegisthus
> Will make you suffer for this insolence.

ELECTRA:
> So. In a rage. You said I could speak freely,
> And now you cannot bear to listen to me.

CLYTEMNESTRA:
> Will you stop talking, ever? I let you speak.
> Can I not even make my sacrifice?

ELECTRA:
> Yes, certainly. Begin your offering,
> And do not blame my tongue. I will be silent.

CLYTEMNESTRA (*to her attendant, with a gesture toward an altar*):
> You there, life up my gift of many fruits
> That I may supplicate this king to grant me   590
> Deliverance from these present fears of mine.
> Hear thou my words, Apollo, our defender,
> Though I must veil their meaning, for I speak
> With no friends near, nor should I bring to light
> The secrets of my heart while she is here
> With her malicious tongue eager to fill
> Mycenae with a reckless flood of rumors.
> But hear me. I can speak no other way.
> O Lycian king, if that perplexing vision
> I saw in last night's dreams was a good omen,   600
> Grant that it be fulfilled; if it was evil,
> Let it recoil upon my enemies.
> If any are now treacherously plotting
> To hurl me from my high estate, prevent them.
> Grant, rather, that unharmed I may still rule

The house of Atreus, sharing my well-being
With those friends who are sharing it today,
And with those children who have not pursued me
With bitterness and hatred. Lord Apollo,
Be gracious to us, hear this prayer, and grant us   610
What we have asked. And as for what remains,
I am convinced that thou, a god, must know it,
Although I hold my tongue; for surely nothing
Escapes the knowledge of the sons of Zeus.

Enter OLD MAN

OLD MAN:

Ladies, I am a stranger. May I ask
If this is the palace of the King, Aegisthus?

CHORUS:

Yes, you have guessed correctly, sir. It is.

OLD MAN:

And am I right? This lady is his wife?
Certainly she is royal in appearance.

CHORUS:

Yes, you are right. You stand before the Queen.   620

OLD MAN:

Madam. (*bowing*) I bring to you and King Aegisthus
News from a friend you will be glad to hear.

CLYTEMNESTRA:

I welcome the good omen of your words.
But first I wish to know who sent you to us.

OLD MAN:

The Phocian Phanoteus. An urgent matter.

CLYTEMNESTRA:

What is it? Tell me. Coming from a friend,
Your message will undoubtedly be pleasant.

OLD MAN:

In brief, it comes to this. Orestes is dead.

ELECTRA:

Oh! Oh! I cannot bear it! I am lost!

CLYTEMNESTRA (*to* OLD MAN):

What? What was that? Pay no attention to her.   630

OLD MAN:

I said and say again: Orestes is dead.

ELECTRA:

I am lost, lost! My life is utterly ruined!

CLYTEMNESTRA (*to* ELECTRA):

Mind your own business. Now, sir, let me know
All the details. How did he come to die?

OLD MAN:

I was sent here to tell you everything.
Orestes went to that great festival
The Delphian games, the glory of all Greece.
When the loud call announced the first event,
A foot-race, he came in, a brilliant figure
That all men marveled at; and when he had run   640
Back to the starting point, he made his exit
Crowned with the splendid prize of victory.
To make the account of all his triumphs brief,
I only say I have never known his equal.
But I should add this much: he was the winner
Of every contest called for by the judges.
Men thought him happy, hearing him proclaimed
Time and again: an Argive named Orestes,
Son of King Agamemnon, who once gathered
The famous host of Greece. Up to this point   650
All had gone well, but when a god strikes, no one,
However strong, escapes. Another day,
When the swift chariots were to race at dawn,
He was among the many charioteers
Who entered: one was an Achaean; one
From Sparta; two from Libya, skilled in guiding
The car with its yoked horses; fifth among them
Orestes came, driving Thessalian mares;
The sixth, with chestnut colts, was from Aetolia;
The seventh a Magnesian; and the eighth   660
An Aenian, with white horses; ninth a man
From Athens, built by gods; and a Boeotian,
Making the tenth. Then when their lots were drawn,
They took their stations where the officials placed them.
The brazen trumpet sounded and they started,
Shaking their reins and shouting at their horses,
Filling the whole course with the noise of the chariots'
Rumble and rattle. The dust flew up in clouds,
As the men plied their goads in the confusion,
Striving to draw ahead of each others' hubs   670
And snorting teams, who flecked with foam their wheels
And the backs of those in front. Making the turns,
Curbing his left horse, slacking his right-hand rein,
Orestes with his axles almost grazed
The posts that marked the limits of the course.
So far, no chariot had been hurt, but now
The hard-mouthed horses of the Aenian bolted,
And as they turned into the seventh lap,
Swerved and collided head-first with the team

From Barca. Other disasters followed, crash   680
Upon shattering crash, until the Crisan stadium
Was strewn with wrecks. When the Athenian saw
The first mishap, he shrewdly turned aside
And paused, letting the chariots surge past him
Like a tumultuous wave. Orestes, holding
His horses back, relying on the finish,
Was driving last; but when he saw that no one
Remained but the Athenian, with a cry
That rang in the ears of his swift colts, he followed
Till he drew even. Then the two raced on,   690
First one man's head in front and then the other's.
Through each remaining round wretched Orestes
Stood steady in his steady chariot,
Driving in safety, but at last he slackened
His left rein while the horses were still turning
So that before he knew it his hub struck
The edge of the post and broke. Caught in the reins,
He was thrown out over the chariot-rail,
And as he fell to the ground, his colts ran wild
Into the middle of the course. The crowd,   700
Seeing that he had fallen, gave a cry
Of pity for a youth who had done so much
And had met so sad an end, now dashed to the earth,
Now tossed feet-foremost to the sky. At last
The other drivers managed to bring to a halt
His runaway horses and untangled him,
So bathed in blood, so broken, so disfigured
That no friend would have known him. They lost no time
In burning him, and envoys of the Phocians
Are on their way here with the pitiful ashes   710
Of his great body in a little urn
For burial at home. That is my story,
Sad if mere words are sad. But when he died,
Those of us who were present thought the sight
Sadder than anything we had ever seen.

CHORUS:
It is unbearable! Our kings are gone;
Their ancient race has perished root and branch.

CLYTEMNESTRA:
O Zeus! Is this good news? Or fearful news
That works to my advantage? It is bitter
To owe my life to my calamities.   720

OLD MAN:
Madam, why has this news disheartened you?

CLYTEMNESTRA:
What mystery is in motherhood! No mother
Can hate her child, no matter how she is wronged.

OLD MAN:
>Well then, our coming seems entirely useless.

CLYTEMNESTRA:
>No, no, not useless. How can you say that,
>When you have brought me sure proof of his death?
>I gave him life, suckled him, nurtured him,
>Yet he forsook me and forsook his country
>To live in exile, never seeing me,
>Reproaching me with the murder of his father,   730
>Threatening me with such terrible retribution
>That night or day I could not sleep in comfort,
>But every moment lived in fear of death.
>But now I am no longer filled with fear
>Of him or of this girl, this worse affliction,
>Draining my very life-blood while she lived
>In my own home. After today she cannot
>Make any threat that could disturb my peace.

ELECTRA:
>Oh, oh! What misery! And you, Orestes,
>How pitiful! Mocked, taunted by your mother   740
>When you are as you are! Should such things be?

CLYTEMNESTRA:
>You are not as you should be, but he is.

ELECTRA:
>Nemesis hear! He has just died! Avenge him!

CLYTEMNESTRA:
>She *has* avenged one who deserved her justice.

ELECTRA:
>Of course! Insult us now that you have triumphed!

CLYTEMNESTRA:
>You will not stop me, then? You and Orestes?

ELECTRA:
>How could we stop you? We ourselves are silenced.

CLYTEMNESTRA:
>Sir, you should be rewarded for your coming
>If you have really silenced all her clamor.

OLD MAN:
>If things have gone well, I had better leave.   750

CLYTEMNESTRA:
>No, by no means. To let you go would be
>Unworthy of me and of the friend who sent you.
>Come in, and let this girl stay here outside
>To wail her friends' afflictions and her own.

>>*Exeunt* CLYTEMNESTRA *and* OLD MAN

ELECTRA:
>What a grief-stricken mother! What distress!
>You noticed her? How freely her tears flowed
>When she bewailed her son and mourned his fate?

Why, when she left us, she was laughing. Brother,
Your dying has destroyed me. Dear Orestes,
You have torn from my heart my one remaining hope,   760
The hope that you might live to avenge, some day,
Your father and your miserable sister.
Where shall I turn now? I am all alone,
Robbed of my father and of you. I see
Nothing ahead but slavery with those
Whom I hate most, the murderers of my father.
Can this be right? But I will never again
Live with them, or set foot inside that house.
No. I will lie down at these gates, and here
Waste away, friendless. And if those inside   770
Are angry, let them kill me. Death is sweet,
But life so cruel I want no more of it.

CHORUS:
Where are the bolts of Zeus, the rays of Apollo?
Do the gods look on and do nothing to punish evil?

EL.: (*weeping*):   Oh! Oh!
CH.:   Why do you weep so long?
EL.: (*as if accusing the gods*):   Ah! Ah! CHORUS: Hush! Hush!
Do not be reckless, Electra.

EL.:   No more! CHORUS: Child, what is wrong?
EL.:   Beyond all doubt he is dead.
If you tell me to hope, you make my sorrow more bitter,   780
You crush my heart with your tread.

CHORUS:
But Ámphiaráus died, betrayed by a woman
For a golden necklace; yet even so, in Hades —

EL.: (*weeping*):   Oh! Oh!
CH.:   Still he continues to reign.
EL.:   Oh! Oh! CHORUS: You may well weep, for the woman who
killed him —

EL.:   Was slain. CHORUS: Ah yes. *She* was slain.
EL.:   I know, I know! For a son
Came to avenge him. But I — have I an avenger?
No. I have none now, none.   790

CHORUS:
Poor girl, how pitiable has been your fate!

EL.:   Too well, too well I know it. Like a flood
Of sorrow is my life, dark, wild, and dreadful,
A year-long torrent.

CH.:   Yes. We have seen your grief and understood.
EL.:   Do not mislead me then. It is too late
For any hope of comfort. CHORUS: Oh, Electra!

EL.:   No happiness can come now from my brother,
The son of my great father.

CH.:   Death is the lot appointed for mankind.   800
EL.:   But not a death like his, for he died caught
         Fast in the tangled reins, dragged down, and trampled
             By galloping horses.
CH.:   Calamity beyond the reach of thought!
EL.:   Beyond all thought. His ashes are consigned
         To earth in a far country — CHORUS: Cruel, cruel!
EL.:   Without my hands to pour libations for him,
             Without my tears to mourn him.
                                   Enter CHRYSOTHEMIS

CHRYSOTHEMIS:
         Dear sister! I am hurrying back too happy
         To care about propriety. I have   810
         Wonderful news for you, news that will end
         All your long sorrows, all your suffering.
ELECTRA:
         Why, where could you find help for me? What end
         Can possibly be imagined for my pain?
CHRYSOTHEMIS:
         Listen, Electra! He has come — Orestes! —
         As surely as you see me standing here.
ELECTRA:
         Orestes! Poor girl, have you lost your senses?
         Or are you making fun of our misfortunes?
CHRYSOTHEMIS:
         I! Sneer at you? Oh sister, no! I swear it!
         I tell you he is here with us himself.   820
ELECTRA:
         Ah! Who has told you that? What have you heard
         That you have been so ready to believe?
CHRYSOTHEMIS:
         What I believe is not what someone told me
         But what I saw myself. I have clear proof.
ELECTRA:
         Proof? Certainty? Child, child, what have you seen
         That could have filled you with such feverish hope?
CHRYSOTHEMIS:
         First hear my story — I beg you by the gods —
         Before you say that I am wise or foolish.
ELECTRA:
         Well, let me hear it, if that comforts you.
CHRYSOTHEMIS:
         You shall hear everything. When I had reached   830
         Our father's tomb, I saw that milk had flowed
         Down its old mound a little while before,
         And that the burial place was wreathed with flowers

99

Of every kind. All that astonished me,
And I looked round, afraid that someone else
Was near me, but the silence was unbroken.
Then I crept nearer to the tomb, and there
On the mound's edge I saw a lock of hair
Cut only recently. That very moment
There flashed upon me the familiar image   840
Of dear Orestes, dearer than all the world,
Sure evidence that the lock belonged to him.
I took it up in silence, reverently,
But my eyes overflowed with tears of joy.
I am as certain now as I was then
This splendid tribute must have come from him.
Except for you and me who else is there
Who would perform that duty? And I know
I did not do it, nor did you. How could you?
You would be punished if you left the house   850
Even to worship the gods. As for our mother,
When could she do such things without our knowledge?
When has she ever wished to do them? No.
Orestes left these offerings at the tomb.
Take courage, dear Electra! No one lives
His whole life long ruled by one changeless fortune.
We have endured great misery, but today
Perhaps will prove the dawn of happiness.

ELECTRA:
How sad, how sad that you should know so little!

CHRYSOTHEMIS:
What do you mean? Can such news be unwelcome?   860

ELECTRA:
You do not know how far astray you are.

CHRYSOTHEMIS:
Surely I know what I have seen myself.

ELECTRA:
Orestes is dead, poor child. Do not expect
Deliverance from him; that hope is gone.

CHRYSOTHEMIS:
Oh! Oh! How cruel! Where did you hear that?

ELECTRA:
I heard it from a man who saw him die.

CHRYSOTHEMIS:
And where is *he*? This is bewildering.

ELECTRA:
Inside. Our mother's guest — and not unwelcome.

CHRYSOTHEMIS:
No! No! But then, who is responsible
For all those honors paid to our father's tomb?   870

ELECTRA:
>Someone, I think, who acted for Orestes;
>The honors were in memory of his death.

CHRYSOTHEMIS:
>I cannot bear it! I came hurrying here
>To bring good news, not knowing the full extent
>Of our calamities, but now I find
>All the old sorrow and new grief as well.

ELECTRA:
>Yes, so you think; but if you listen to me,
>You will make lighter the heavy load we bear.

CHRYSOTHEMIS:
>Am I to bring the dead to life again?

ELECTRA:
>I did not mean that. I am not so foolish.   880

CHRYSOTHEMIS:
>Then what do you ask of me? What can I do?

ELECTRA:
>You can be brave and follow my advice.

CHRYSOTHEMIS:
>Of course I will give you whatever help I can.

ELECTRA:
>Remember that success is never easy.

CHRYSOTHEMIS:
>I know, and I will do my utmost for you.

ELECTRA:
>Then you must hear the plan I intend to follow.
>You know as well as I that we have no friends
>To give us their support. They are all dead,
>And we two are alone. While I had news
>Orestes was alive, I kept up hope   890
>That he would come to avenge our father's murder,
>But now that he is gone I look to you.
>Have courage enough to help your sister kill
>The murderer of our father, kill Aegisthus.
>I can keep no secret from you now. How long
>Will you remain content with doing nothing?
>What can you see to hope for? You can only
>Grieve for your lost inheritance, and lament
>That you are unmarried and are growing old
>Without a bridal song. You cannot hope   900
>To marry now. Aegisthus is not stupid;
>He never will allow you to have children.
>A child of yours — or mine — would be his ruin.
>But do what I advise. Then you will win
>The praise of our dead father and our brother
>For showing piety; and win the name

Of a free woman, true daughter of your house,
Through all the years to come. Then you will find
The husband that you deserve, for all men prize
Greatness of character. Surely you see   910
How famous you and I will both become
If you will only listen to what I say.
No one who sees us, citizen or stranger,
Will fail to greet and praise us: "These, my friends,
Are the sisters who preserved their father's house,
Who, when their foes had carried all before them,
Were ready to risk their lives by taking murder
Into their own hands. These two are entitled
To all the love and reverence we can give them.
At every festival and public gathering   920
We should pay tribute to their bravery."
So will men speak of us, alive or dead;
Through the whole world our fame will last forever.
Dear sister, listen! Support your father, share
Your brother's burden. Free me and free yourself
From these afflictions. And remember this:
A base life brings the nobly born to shame.

CHORUS:
One should be cautious, in a case like this,
Both in advising and in being advised.

CHRYSOTHEMIS:
My friends, she would have shown much better judgment   930
Than she has shown, if she had stopped to think
Before she said a word. (*to* ELECTRA) What has induced you
To arm yourself for battle with such boldness,
And call on me to help you? Have you forgotten
You are a woman and not a man? You cannot
Match the resources of your enemies.
Fortune for them continues at the flood;
For us it ebbs away, and fades to nothing.
Who could consider killing a man like him,
And not pay dearly for it? Oh, be careful!   940
Bad as things are for us, they could be worse,
If anyone should hear what you have said.
Our fame will bring no comfort when we die
An ignominious death. Merely to die
Is not the worst; the worst is to long to die
And not be able to. Sister! I beg you,
Control yourself before we are utterly ruined,
Before our family is destroyed forever.
I will not breathe a word of what you have said,
I will not act upon it. And as for you,   950
Admit at long last that the part of wisdom
Is for the weak to give way to the strong.

CHORUS:
> Electra, she is right. Nothing in life
> Brings greater profit than far-sighted prudence.

ELECTRA:
> I expected you to say that. I was sure
> You would refuse what I proposed. So then,
> I must do this thing myself and by myself,
> For I am determined that it shall be done.

CHRYSOTHEMIS:
> I wish you had shown that spirit on the day
> Our father died. What could have stopped your triumph?   960

ELECTRA:
> I was no different then, but saw less clearly.

CHRYSOTHEMIS:
> Try to see always just as you saw then.

ELECTRA:
> That means you will take no part in what I am doing.

CHRYSOTHEMIS:
> It does. The attempt may end in utter failure.

ELECTRA:
> I admire your wisdom, hate your cowardice.

CHRYSOTHEMIS:
> I will be no less patient when you praise me.

ELECTRA:
> You will never have to hear *me* praising you.

CHRYSOTHEMIS:
> Well, we shall see. The time ahead is long.

ELECTRA:
> Go! Go away! You cannot possibly help me.

CHRYSOTHEMIS:
> Yes, I could help, but you refuse to listen.   970

ELECTRA:
> Run to your mother. Tell her everything.

CHRYSOTHEMIS:
> My hatred is not strong enough for that.

ELECTRA:
> At least you understand how much you wrong me.

CHRYSOTHEMIS:
> Wrong you! My only thought is how to help you.

ELECTRA:
> To do right, then, I have to follow you?

CHRYSOTHEMIS:
> When you see clearly, you will lead us both.

ELECTRA:
> How strange to be so eloquent and so wrong!

CHRYSOTHEMIS:
> A good description of your own behavior.

ELECTRA:
> What! Is the cause I advocate not just?

CHRYSOTHEMIS:
> A just cause can be dangerous at times.   980

ELECTRA:
> That is a rule I do not care to live by.

CHRYSOTHEMIS:
> If you keep on, you will come to think as I do.

ELECTRA:
> I *will* keep on. You have not frightened me.

CHRYSOTHEMIS:
> Are you sure? You will not listen to my advice?

ELECTRA:
> There is nothing that is worse than bad advice.

CHRYSOTHEMIS:
> It seems, then, that we disagree completely.

ELECTRA:
> I made my mind up long ago, not now.

CHRYSOTHEMIS:
> Then I will go. You cannot bring yourself
> To accept my words, nor I to accept your thinking.

ELECTRA:
> Very well, go. I will never follow you   990
> No matter how much you may want me to.
> It is sheer folly to cherish an illusion.

CHRYSOTHEMIS:
> Since you are so convinced of your own wisdom,
> Do as you please; but when the worst has happened,
> You will come to understand that I was right.

> > *Exit* CHRYSOTHEMIS

CHORUS:
> The birds of the air, with their unfailing instinct,
> > Cherish in turn the birds who gave them birth;
> > Seeing their care, why cannot we on earth
> Repay our self-same debts in equal measure?
> > By the fierce lightning flung by Zeus's hand,   1000
> > By Themis, throned in heaven, those who stand
> Convicted shall not long escape unpunished.
> O voice that reaches to the world beneath us,
> > Let the dead hear you pitifully wail.
> Bring to the son of Atreus there in Hades
> > Your sad and shameful tale.

> Say that the fortunes of his house are fallen,
> > Its daily harmony of child with child

Broken by discord, harsh, unreconciled;
Say that forsaken, alone in this storm of sorrow,   1010
     Electra never ceases to bewail
     Her father's murder, like the nightingale,
Who pours out endlessly its lamentation.
Once she has rid her house of its two furies,
     Indifferent to life, she goes indifferent to death.
Will a child so noble, so true to a noble father
     Ever again draw breath?

No man of honor wants to cloud his fame
By a base life, and die without a name.
     So you, my daughter, wish to spend your days   1020
Mourning with those who mourn, that you may be
Known for your wisdom and your piety,
     Shunning reproach to win a twofold praise.

I pray that you may come at last to tower
Above your enemies in wealth and power,
     Although today they crush you to the ground;
For even now you reverence Zeus the king,
And the great laws of his establishing,
     So that your anguish is with honor crowned.

                         Enter ORESTES *and* PYLADES

ORESTES:
     Ladies, have we been given the right directions?   1030
     Will this road take us to our destination?
CHORUS:
     And where is that, sir? What has brought you here?
ORESTES:
     I wish to find the palace of Aegisthus.
CHORUS:
     Well, you have found it. You were not misled.
ORESTES:
     They have been looking forward to our arrival.
     Will one of you go tell them we are here?
CHORUS (*indicating* ELECTRA):
     Yes, she will go, if one of the family should.
ORESTES:
     Madam, will you be good enough to say
     The men from Phocis ask to see Aegisthus?
ELECTRA:
     Sir, are you bringing evidence — ah, dreadful! —   1040
     To prove the truth of the rumor we have heard?
ORESTES:
     I know nothing of any rumor. Stróphius
     Sent me to give the news about Orestes.

ELECTRA:
>What is your news? How terrified I am!

ORESTES:
>We are bringing, as you can see, in this small urn
>The little that is left of his dead body.

ELECTRA:
>It is too clear! An unendurable sight,
>This grievous burden here before my eyes!

ORESTES:
>If your tears flow for what Orestes suffered,
>You have to know this urn contains his dust. 1050

ELECTRA:
>Then let me hold it, I implore you, sir,
>If he is hidden there, that I may weep
>Over his ashes, that I may lament
>Not for myself alone but my whole race.

ORESTES:
>Give her the urn. She cannot be asking for it,
>Whoever she is, out of ill-will. No doubt
>She is a friend, or member of his family.

>>*The urn is given to* ELECTRA

ELECTRA:
>I loved you best in all the world, Orestes,
>And only this remains of what I loved,
>Your sole memorial. When you left home, 1060
>I had high hopes. How differently I greet you
>On your return! I sent away a child
>Splendid with promise. Now I hold you, nothing,
>Here in my hands. I would that I had died
>Before I saved you, kept you from being murdered,
>And spirited you away to a strange land.
>You would have been struck down on the same day,
>And shared your father's tomb; but as it is,
>You perished miserably, far from your country,
>Exiled from home, without your sister near you. 1070
>I weep to think these loving hands of mine
>Could not perform their office, could not wash
>Or dress your body, or from the consuming fire
>Lift this sad load. No! Strangers honored you,
>My poor Orestes; so you come back to me,
>A little dust shut in a little urn.
>I weep to think of all the care I gave you
>In bygone days — a hard task that was sweet —
>And gave in vain. Your mother never loved you
>As much as I did; I was your only nurse; 1080

I was the one whom you called sister. Now,
All this is ended in a single day,
For you are dead, and you have swept away
Everything with you, like a hurricane.
Our father is no more; my life is over,
Since you are gone from me; our enemies laugh;
And our unnatural mother is mad with joy.
You often sent me messages in secret
To say you would come to take your vengeance on her.
But destiny, your evil lot and mine,   1090
Has taken everything, and sent you home
Not in the human form I loved so well,
But only ashes and an empty shade.
My poor Orestes! Oh, my dear, my dear!
Yours was a grievous journey back to me.
Oh, brother! You have utterly destroyed me.
Then take me to your home, my nothingness
To yours; let me forever live with you
In the underworld. When you were here on earth
We shared alike, and now I long to die,   1100
Not to be parted from you in the grave,
For I can see the dead are free from pain.

CHORUS:
Your father was a mortal man, Electra.
So was Orestes. Do not weep too much.
This is a debt that all of us must pay.

ORESTES:
What shall I say? Where can I find the words?
Yet I must speak. I cannot restrain myself.

ELECTRA:
What is the matter? Why did you say that?

ORESTES:
Are you Electra? The renowned Electra?

ELECTRA:
I am — and in the utmost misery.   1110

ORESTES:
Ah! Such misfortune has been hard to bear.

ELECTRA:
Sir, surely you are not concerned for *me?*

ORESTES:
Treated so cruelly and irreverently!

ELECTRA:
You say harsh things of me, and they are true.

ORESTES:
To have lived unmarried and so sick at heart!

ELECTRA:
> What does your fixed look mean? And your laments?

ORESTES:
> How little I have known of my own sorrow!

ELECTRA:
> What have I said to give you that impression?

ORESTES:
> I have seen the greatness of your suffering.

ELECTRA:
> You have seen no more than a small part of it.   1120

ORESTES:
> But how can anything be worse than this?

ELECTRA:
> To live in the home of murderers, that is worse.

ORESTES:
> Who has been killed? What murderers do you mean?

ELECTRA:
> My father's. And I am forced to be their slave.

ORESTES:
> Who has subjected you to slavery?

ELECTRA:
> A mother, who has the name and nothing else.

ORESTES:
> How has she done it? By violence, or ill-treatment?

ELECTRA:
> Violence, ill-treatment, every sort of outrage.

ORESTES:
> Is there no one to help you? No one to interfere?

ELECTRA:
> Not now. There was once. I have been given his ashes.   1130

ORESTES:
> Such pain as yours is pitiful to see.

ELECTRA:
> You are the first who ever pitied me.

ORESTES:
> No one has come till now who suffered with you.

ELECTRA:
> Are you some kinsman? Where is it you come from?

ORESTES (*indicating* CHORUS):
> I will answer you if they are friends of yours.

ELECTRA:
> Yes, they are friends. They can be fully trusted.

ORESTES:
> Then give me back the urn and I will tell you.

ELECTRA:
> Oh no! Not that! Do not ask that of me!

ORESTES:

    Do what I say, and you will not go wrong.

ELECTRA:

    Have pity! Do not take my greatest treasure!   1140

ORESTES:

    You must not keep it. ELECTRA: How I grieve, dear brother,
    If I am not to give you burial!

ORESTES:

    Hush! Do not speak so. You have no right to mourn.

ELECTRA:

    I have no right to mourn for my dead brother?

ORESTES:

    No right to speak of him as you have done.

ELECTRA:

    Why not? Has my dead brother so disowned me?

ORESTES:

    No one disowns you, but you must not grieve.

ELECTRA:

    Of course I must. These are Orestes' ashes.

ORESTES:

    No, they are not. That tale is only fiction.

ELECTRA:

    Then where is my unhappy brother buried?   1150

ORESTES:

    Nowhere at all. The living are not buried.

ELECTRA:

    What! What is that you said? ORESTES: Nothing untrue.

ELECTRA:

    Orestes is alive? ORESTES: If I am, yes.

ELECTRA:

    You? Is it you? ORESTES: Look at my father's ring,
    This signet, and decide if I speak the truth.

ELECTRA:

    What utter happiness! ORESTES: Yes, it is perfect.

ELECTRA:

    Is this your voice I hear? ORESTES: My very own.

ELECTRA:

    I am holding you? ORESTES: Never to let me go.

ELECTRA:

    Look, my dear friends, my fellow citizens!
    Here is Orestes! His death was a mere trick,   1160
    A trick allowing him to get here safely.

CHORUS:

    We see him, child, and our eyes overflow
    With tears of happiness for your good fortune.

ELECTRA:

                    Dear, dear Orestes!

        His son! The son of my dearest father!

        You have come at last. You are with me.

        You have found me, seen me. This is what you have longed for.
ORES.: Yes, I am here. But hush! Say nothing yet.
EL.:   What do you mean?
ORES.: Silence is best. Someone inside might hear.   1170
EL.:   Now by immortal Artemis, the virgin!

            I would never stoop to be frightened

            By a household of useless women, forever

                Burdening the earth.
ORES.: Do not forget that women too are warlike.

        I know you have had convincing proof of that.
EL.:   Yes, cruel! Cruel!

            You waken the memory of bitter sorrow,

                That can never be hidden,

            Grief that can never be done away with,   1180

                That can never release me.
ORES.: I know this too. And yet do not remind us

        Of what took place till the right moment comes.
ELECTRA:

            But the right moment

        To protest, to complain, to make my outcry

            Is every moment, is always!

        And only now have my lips been given their freedom.
ORES.: Yes, I agree. And therefore guard your freedom.
EL.:   What shall I do?
ORES.: Be patient. Say little when speaking is unwise.   1190
EL.:   But who could be silent now instead of speaking?

            When I see you again before me,

            A sight beyond all expectation,

                Beyond all hope.
ORES.: You saw the sight when the gods brought me here.

                *   *   *   *   *   *   *   *   *   *   *

EL.:   What a blessing you speak of!

        Nothing so splendid has ever happened!

                If a god has brought you

            Here to our house, then surely, surely   1200

                The gods are at work here.
ORES.: I have no wish to stop you from rejoicing,

        Yet I am frightened by excessive joy.

ELECTRA:

        At last I am happy! At last you have felt you could come
                here!

But now you have seen the full depth of my suffering
    Do not, do not —
ORES.: What do you ask of me? ELECTRA: Never again deprive
    me
Of the joy of seeing your face.
ORES.: How angry I would be if someone tried to!
EL.: Then you will do what I ask you?   1210
ORES.:   Of course I will.
EL.: Oh, my friends! My friends! When I heard his voice,
    Which I never again could have hoped to hear,
      How could I be still?
  How could I not cry out? How could I not rejoice?
    You have come back to me.
  I see your dear face shining here before me,
    The face I have never forgotten,
      Even in my misery.

ORESTES:

  Say nothing more now than is necessary.   1220
  Our mother's wickedness, the senseless waste,
  Luxury and extravagance of Aegisthus,
  Draining our father's wealth: all that would be
  Too long a story. Tell me this instead:
  What should we do — show ourselves openly,
  Or stay in hiding? What is the surest way
  To silence the mockery of our enemies?
  Then too, when we go in, you must not let
  Your radiant face betray you to your mother.
  Pretend to weep for my reported death,   1230
  And after we have won our victory,
  We will have time for laughter and rejoicing.

ELECTRA:

  Dear brother, I will do what you think right.
  This happiness of mine is not my own.
  You gave it me; and nothing would induce me
  To let you suffer from it even a little,
  However great my benefit. I owe
  The immortal power who now is helping us
  Greater respect than that. You know, I am sure,
  The state of things: Aegisthus is away,   1240
  Our mother is at home. You need not fear
  That she will ever see me with a smile
  Lighting my face, for my long-standing hate
  Has bitten deep. And now that I have seen you,
  I will still weep, weep tears of happiness.
  How can I help it, seeing you come home
  Dead and then living in a single day?

You have so shaken me that if my father
Came back to life, I would not think it strange;
I would believe I saw him. Since your coming   1250
Is no less wonderful, I will be governed
By any wish of yours. If I had been
Alone, I would have either saved myself
Triumphantly or died a noble death.

ORESTES:

Electra! Hush! Someone inside the house
Is at the door. ELECTRA (*to* ORESTES *and* PYLADES): Come
    in, and welcome, strangers.
All the more welcome since what you are bringing
Must be received, though it can give no joy.

                Enter the OLD MAN

OLD MAN:

What utter folly! Have you both lost your senses?
Does life mean nothing to you? You are not standing   1260
On the edge of mortal peril, you are standing
In the very midst of it, as you must know.
If all this time I had not stayed on guard
Behind the door, your plans would have been inside
Before you were yourselves. But as it is,
My caution has protected you from that.
Stop all this talking, all these endless cries
Of happiness and go inside. Delay
Is dangerous at such a time as this.
We should act now and end the business quickly.   1270

ORESTES:

What will my chances be when I go in?

OLD MAN:

You run no risk of being recognized.

ORESTES:

You have told them, then, that I am not alive?

OLD MAN:

They think you are dead. You can be sure of that.

ORESTES:

Are they pleased to hear such news? What do they say?

OLD MAN:

I will tell you later. Meanwhile things are going
Beautifully for them, even what is ugly.

ELECTRA:

Who is this man, Orestes? Tell me. Please.

ORESTES:

You cannot see? ELECTRA: I cannot even guess.

ORESTES:

You gave me once to a man. You do not know him?   1280

ELECTRA:

    What man? What are you saying? ORESTES: You had
          arranged
    To have me taken secretly to Phocis.

ELECTRA:

    Is this my only friend? The only man
    Loyal to me the day they killed our father?

ORESTES:

    He is the one. But ask me no more questions.

ELECTRA:

    O day of crowning happiness! O friend,
    Who single-handed saved our father's house!
    To think that you have come! Can it be you
    Who rescued us from suffering and from death,
    Me and my brother? Oh, how dear these hands are!   1290
    What kindly services these feet have done us!
    You, here so long without being recognized!
    Giving no sign, killing me with your story,
    Knowing how sweet the truth was! Welcome, father!
    Yes, I think of you as a father. Welcome!
    I tell you that in one day I have hated
    And loved you more than anyone in the world.

OLD MAN:

    You have said enough, I think. As for the story
    Of all the intervening years, Electra,
    There will be many nights as they wheel round   1300
    And many days to make it clear to you.
    But I say this to you two standing there:
    Now is the time to act. Now Clytemnestra
    Is in the house alone; no man is near her.
    If you delay, remember you will face
    More enemies, who will be better fighters.

ORESTES:

    Pylades, this is no time for further talk.
    We must go in at once, when we have honored
    My father's gods, whose statues guard his gates.

                Exeunt ORESTES, PYLADES, *and* OLD MAN

ELECTRA:

    O Lord Apollo! Hear them and be gracious.   1310
    And hear me also, who so many times
    Have stood before thee, offering reverently
    Whatever gifts I had. And now I pray thee,
    Lycian Apollo — I can do no more —
    Here on my knees I beg thee: look with favor
    Upon our undertaking. Let men see
    How wickedness is punished by the gods.

                      Exit ELECTRA

CHORUS:

> Look how Ares, breathing out slaughter,
> > Moves invincibly onward! And with him
> > Into the house go the hunters of evil;   1320
> None can escape those hounds' unfailing pursuit.
> > Therefore we know that the dream we cherished
> > Will soon bear fruit.

> The champion of the dead in Hades
> > Creeps with stealth through the door of the palace
> > Filled with his father's ancient treasure.
> Sharp death goes with him and Hermes goes before.
> > The god who hid this deceit in darkness
> > Delays no more.

Enter ELECTRA

ELECTRA:

> O dearest friends! At any moment now   1330
> The men will finish the business. Wait. Be still.

CH.: What are they doing? ELECTRA: Standing close beside
> her
> While she prepares the urn for burial.

CH.: Why have you run outside here? ELECTRA: To make
> sure
> Aegisthus does not take us by surprise.

CLYT.: Help! Help! Not a friend is here in the house!
> It is filled with murderers!

EL.: There! Inside! Did you hear that cry?

CH.: I heard terrible sounds, and shuddered to hear them.

CLYT.: Oh! Oh! Aegisthus, where are you?   1340

EL.: Listen! Another shriek!

CLYT.: Son! Son! Have pity on your mother!

EL.: What pity had you for him or for his father?

CH.: O wretched city and race! The curse that pursued
> you
> Day after day is ended, is ended at last.

CLYT.: They have struck me! ELECTRA: Strike her again if
> you can!

CLYT.: Oh! Oh! Once more! ELECTRA: If only Aegisthus were with
> you!

CH.: The curse is doing its work. The buried are living.
> Blood in repayment for blood is drained from the
> killers
> > By those who have long since died.   1350

Enter ORESTES *and* PYLADES

114

CHORUS:

> Look! There they come! They have made their sacri-
> fice,
> For their hands reek with blood. I cannot blame them.

EL.:   How did things go, Orestes? ORESTES: All went well,
> If Lord Apollo's oracle spoke well.

EL.:   The creature is dead? ORESTES: You need not be afraid
> That your proud mother will ever again insult you.

CH.:   Be careful! There is Aegisthus!

EL.:   Go back, you two! Go back! ORESTES: Where do you see
> him?

EL.:   There. Coming in from the country,
> Light-hearted and at our mercy.   1360

CH.:   Quick! Into the house! You have done well just now.
> May all go well with you a second time.

ORES.: It will. Fear nothing. ELECTRA: Do as you planned, but
> hurry!

ORES.:   Yes. I am gone. (*Exeunt*) ELECTRA: I will attend to
> things here.

CH.:   Speak gently to him in a friendly way
> That he may rush off blindly to his struggle
> With retribution.

Enter AEGISTHUS

AEGISTHUS:

> Where are the Phocian strangers? Who can tell me?
> I understand that they have come with news
> About Orestes: killed in a chariot wreck.   1370
> I am asking you, yes you, who used to be
> So impudent. You are affected most,
> It seems to me. You know and can best tell.

ELECTRA:

> Of course I know. Would I be ignorant
> Of matters that are nearest to my heart?

AEGISTHUS:

> Where have the strangers gone to? Tell me that.

ELECTRA:

> Inside the house. Their hostess has received them.

AEGISTHUS:

> And have they brought us word that he is dead?

ELECTRA:

> Not merely word; they have brought him himself.

AEGISTHUS:

> Then I can see all this with my own eyes?   1380

ELECTRA:

> You can indeed. It is a hideous sight.

AEGISTHUS:

> For once, what you have said has given me pleasure.

115

ELECTRA:

    If you find pleasure, make the most of it.

AEGISTHUS:

    Silence! Hear my command! Throw the gates open.
    Let all the citizens of Argos see,
    So that whoever has been buoyed up
    By empty hopes may now look on the dead,
    And take my bit between his teeth without
    Waiting for punishment to teach him wisdom.

ELECTRA:

    I know my duty. I have learned at last   1390
    To take the side of those who are the stronger.

       The shrouded body of CLYTEMNESTRA *is disclosed,*
          with ORESTES *and* PYLADES *standing beside it*

AEGISTHUS:

    O Zeus, this is clear evidence the gods
    Were jealous. But if retribution follows
    For saying this, then I recall my words.
    Uncover the face, for I should mourn my kindred.

ORESTES:

    No. Lift the shroud yourself. What lies before you
    Is yours to see and speak to with affection.

AEGISTHUS:

    Good. I will follow your suggestion. (*to* ELECTRA): You.
    If Clytemnestra is at home, go call her.

ORESTES:

    You need not look far. She is close to you.   1400
            AEGISTHUS *removes the face cloth*

AEGISTHUS:

    How horrible! ORESTES: Afraid? Of a strange face?

AEGISTHUS:

    What men are you? Whose net has trapped me here?

ORESTES:

    You have not yet discovered? Do you still
    Talk of the living as though they were the dead?

AEGISTHUS:

    Ah! Now I understand you. I am lost,
    For this must be Orestes who is speaking.

ORESTES:

    So good a prophet and so long deceived?

AEGISTHUS:

    I have reached the end. But let me say one thing.

ELECTRA:

    No, brother, no! I beg you by the gods,
    Not one word more! What can a minute's time   1410
    Mean to a man engulfed in misery

And at the point of death? Kill him now, now!
And throw him to the creatures who will give him
A fitting burial, out of our sight.
This is the only thing that can repay me
For all that I have suffered in the past.

ORESTES:

Go in at once. The question we are now
Concerned with is your life and not your speaking.

AEGISTHUS:

Why take me in? If what you do is good,
Why do you need the dark? Why not strike quickly?   1420

ORESTES:

I give the orders. Go inside. The place
You killed my father will be where you die.

AEGISTHUS:

Is this house doomed to witness all the woes
Of Pelops' race now and in years to come?

ORESTES:

It will see yours. That much I prophesy.

AEGISTHUS:

You are a better prophet than your father.

ORESTES:

You talk too much and we delay too long.
Now go. AEGISTHUS: Show me the way. ORESTES: You
                    must go first.

AEGISTHUS:

To keep me from escaping? ORESTES: No. To keep you
From dying as you please. I must make sure   1430
Your death is hard. If all who break the law
Were cut down quickly by the sword of justice
Evil would not be rampant in the world.
                    Exeunt ORESTES *and* AEGISTHUS

CHORUS:

O house of Atreus, desperate was your struggle,
Bitter the suffering through which you passed.
        With this day's enterprise you have found freedom,
        And are made whole at last.

Philoctetes

CHARACTERS IN THE PLAY

PHILOCTETES, *son of* POIAS

ODYSSEUS

NEOPTOLEMUS, *son of* ACHILLES *and lord of Scyros*

HERACLES

SAILOR, *disguised as a merchant*

CHORUS, *the crew of* NEOPTOLEMUS

PHILOCTETES

Scene: *The rocky coast of the island of Lemnos*

Enter ODYSSEUS *and* NEOPTOLEMUS, *with* SAILOR *following*

ODYSSEUS:
    Here is the coast of sea-girt Lemnos. No one
    Lives in this land, no one sets foot on it.
    Son of Achilles, Neoptólemus,
    True son of him who was the noblest Greek,
    I left the Málian here, the son of Poías,
    Long years ago, as my commanders ordered.
    With his foot eaten by a running sore,
    He filled the whole camp with his terrible cries,
    His constant and ill-omened shrieks and groans.
    We could not offer sacrifice in peace   10
    Or pour libations. But why speak of that?
    This is no time for speeches. If he learns
    That I am here, then my whole plot will fail.
    I will never take him. Let us get to work.
    I need your help for what is left to do.
    Look for a cave close by that has two mouths,
    Two warm and sunny seats on a cold day,
    Joined by a passage in the rock through which
    The breeze blows in the summer, bringing sleep.
    To the left, not far below, you may find water   20
    Unless the spring has failed. Go quietly
    And signal to me whether he lives there still,
    Or whether we must hunt him somewhere else.
    I can tell you then what lies ahead of us,
    And once you know that, we can work together.
NEOPTOLEMUS (*climbing*):
    You sent me a short journey, lord Odysseus.
    I see a cave, I think, as you described it.
ODYSSEUS:
    Above you or below? I cannot see it.
NEOPTOLEMUS:
    There. Up above. And I can hear no footsteps.
ODYSSEUS:
    He may be inside sleeping. Go and look.   30
NEOPTOLEMUS (*again climbing*):
    The place is empty. No one to be seen.
ODYSSEUS:
    Is there anything to suggest that it is lived in?

NEOPTOLEMUS:
A heap of leaves pressed flat — a bed perhaps.
ODYSSEUS:
There is nothing else? Nothing at all inside?
NEOPTOLEMUS:
Only a wooden cup, roughly hacked out,
A clumsy job, and stuff to start a fire with.
ODYSSEUS:
You have described the treasures of his house.
NEOPTOLEMUS:
Yes, and look here! Rags drying in the sun,
Foul with the matter from a festering sore.
ODYSSEUS:
That certainly is his home. He must be near.   40
How could he go far, crippled as he is,
With that unhealed infection in his foot?
He has gone to look for food, or for an herb
He knows of somewhere that will ease his pain.
Have your man there keep watch. I cannot let him
Come on me unawares, for he would rather
Get hold of me than of the whole Greek army.
NEOPTOLEMUS:
I will see to it that the path is guarded.

Exit SAILOR
NEOPTOLEMUS *climbs down*

And now go on, if you have more to say.
ODYSSEUS:
Son of Achilles, you have a mission here   50
That calls for more than strength. Be loyal to it.
If you are told some plan you never heard of,
You must still help me. You are here to help.
NEOPTOLEMUS:
What are your orders, then? ODYSSEUS: I want to have
    you
Trick Philoctétes when you talk to him.
When he asks who you are and where you come from,
Tell him Achilles' son — that needs no lie —
But say you are homeward bound, you have left the army
And the Greek ships. You hate them, hate them all,
Who begged you to leave home, since without you   60
They could not capture Troy, but when you came,
Refused your just demand, your father's arms,
Saying you were not worthy, and instead
Handed them over to Odysseus. Call me
Whatever name you choose, however vile.
That will not trouble me, but if you fail us,

122

All of the Greeks will suffer. We must get
His bow from Philoctetes. Otherwise
It lies not in your power to capture Troy.
You see why *you* can safely deal with him   70
When I cannot? Because you will be trusted.
You were not under oath; you were not forced
To sail to Troy, nor had you any part
In the first expedition, but all that
Is true of me. If he should see me, therefore,
While he still has his bow, I am a dead man,
And you too are destroyed. What we must do
Is to contrive some way for you to steal
The invincible weapon. Son, I know your nature.
Lying and trickery are abhorrent to you,   80
But make this effort now, since victory
Is a sweet prize to win. Some other time
We will prove that we are honest, but today
Let me persuade you to give up your scruples
A little while, and then forever after
You can be called the noblest of mankind.

NEOPTOLEMUS:
Son of Laertes, what I cannot bear
Even to hear of I cannot bear to do.
My nature does not lend itself to baseness,
And neither did my father's, so they tell me.   90
I am prepared to take the man by force
But not by cunning. And in any case,
A man with one foot cannot win a fight
Against so many. Since I was sent to help you,
I hate the thought of being called a traitor.
Still, lord Odysseus, I would much prefer
To fail with honor than to win by fraud.

ODYSSEUS:
You are worthy of your father. At your age
I too was slow to speak and quick to act.
But from experience I have learned that men   100
Are mastered by the word and not the deed.

NEOPTOLEMUS:
Your orders come to this: I am to lie.

ODYSSEUS:
You are to use deceit to capture him.

NEOPTOLEMUS:
Why should I use deceit? Why not persuasion?

ODYSSEUS:
He would never listen. Force is useless too.

NEOPTOLEMUS:
Has he such terrible strength that he is fearless?

123

ODYSSEUS:
His deadly arrows never miss their mark.
NEOPTOLEMUS:
So it is risky even to go near him?
ODYSSEUS:
Yes, without using trickery, as I said.
NEOPTOLEMUS:
Lying is not disgraceful, then, you think? 110
ODYSSEUS:
No, not if we can save ourselves by lying.
NEOPTOLEMUS:
But could I face him when I said such things?
ODYSSEUS:
It is wrong to hang back when you stand to gain.
NEOPTOLEMUS:
What would I gain if he should come to Troy?
ODYSSEUS:
We cannot capture Troy without his bow.
NEOPTOLEMUS:
And yet they said I was to capture it.
ODYSSEUS:
You and the bow together, not alone.
NEOPTOLEMUS:
In that case, I must get my hands on it.
ODYSSEUS:
If you succeed, you will receive two prizes.
NEOPTOLEMUS:
Let me know what they are, and I consent. 120
ODYSSEUS:
You will be called not only wise but brave.
NEOPTOLEMUS:
Well, I will do it. I will curb my conscience.
ODYSSEUS:
You remember my advice? You mean to take it?
NEOPTOLEMUS:
Of course, since I have just agreed to act.
ODYSSEUS:
Stay where you are, then, till he comes this way.
I cannot let him see me. I will leave,
And have our lookout there rejoin the ship.
And if it seems to me that you are taking
Too long a time here, I will send him back
Dressed as a merchant-skipper. This disguise 130
Will make things easier, for Philoctetes
Will never know him, and the man will tell
Some clever story. Take your cues from him.
Now I will go. The rest is in your hands,
And may the guide of mortals, crafty Hermes,

Lead us, and Victory, and Athena, goddess
Guarding our country, who preserves me always.

Exit ODYSSEUS
Enter CHORUS *of sailors*

CHORUS:

Strange is this country. Here we are strangers.
What shall we hide, for the man suspects us?
 What shall we say?   140
Counsel us, sir. In skill and wisdom
Unmatched is the prince to whom Zeus has given
 A scepter's godlike sway.
And to you this sovereign power has descended
From days long past. Then how can we serve you?
 Show us the way.

NEOPTOLEMUS:

Here are his quarters, close by the water.
Look for yourselves, if you wish to see them.
You have nothing to fear, the place is empty;
But as soon as that dread man makes his way homeward   150
Come when you see me give you a signal
And help in whatever way you can.

CHORUS:

We have always watched for a way to help you.
Beyond every other concern your safety
 Has been our care.
What kind of place has he found for shelter?
He might catch us off-guard and attack us. We surely
 Should know where he is, and beware.
What home does he have? What path does he follow?
Has he gone away, or is he resting   160
 Inside his lair?

NEO.:   This is his house with its double doorways,
This rocky cave where he sleeps. Come see it.
CH.:   Where has the wretched creature gone to?
NEO.:   I am very sure he is near here somewhere,
Slowly dragging himself along,
Searching for something to eat, poor fellow.
That is the life they say he is living,
Hunting for game with his feathered arrows,
And no one comes near to heal his pain.   170

CHORUS:

Truly I pity him. Think how he suffers,
 Never beholding a friendly face,
Racked by disease and with none to tend him,
 Bewildered day after lonely day

By his thronging hardships. How can he bear them?
　The ways of the gods are hard to trace.
Ah! men whose lot exceeds due measure,
　How steeped in woe are they!

This noble son of an ancient household —
　No one, perhaps, more highly born —　　　　　　　180
Is bereft of all that life can offer.
　With dappled and shaggy beasts he lies,
Hungry, in anguish beyond all curing,
　Lone, friendless, utterly forlorn.
And only a distant mountain echo
　Answers his bitter cries.

NEOPTOLEMUS:
　There is nothing strange in all that has happened,
For if I can judge, the gods are at work here.
The wrath of relentless Chrysé inflicted
The first of the torments from which he suffered.　　190
And as for the woe he now endures
With none to help him, some god has willed it
That he may not bend on Troy his resistless
God-given bow before the day
Shall come on which to that same weapon
The city, men say, is destined to fall.

CHORUS:
　Hush, hush! NEOPTOLEMUS: What is it? CHORUS: Listen!
　　　a sudden outcry
　Like that of someone in lifelong pain.
Over there — or there. The sound is fearful,
　The voice of a man who is struggling to walk. Again　200
That distant anguish. I cannot mistake it,
　It is too plain.

We must plan. NEOPTOLEMUS: Plan what? CHORUS: Some-
　　　thing new. He is almost upon us.
　Not with glad pipes is he drawing near,
Like a shepherd home from the fields, but moaning,
　Perhaps when he saw the empty roadstead appear,
Perhaps at a stab of pain when he stumbled.
　　How awful to hear!

　　　　　　　　　　　　　　Enter PHILOCTETES

PHILOCTETES:
　Strangers, who are you? What land have you come from?
Why have you put in here? There is no harbor,　　　　210
No house on all this coast. What is your race?
What is your city? The clothes you wear are Greek,

A style I love. If only you would talk!
I look like some wild beast, but do not shrink,
Do not be frightened. Have compassion on me,
For I am wretched, lonely, destitute.
My pain is terrible. I have no friends.
Speak, if you come as friends. O speak to me!
We ought at least to talk to one another.

NEOPTOLEMUS:

Then, sir, I tell you first that we are Greeks.   220
That is the thing you wanted most to know.

PHILOCTETES:

How wonderful a sound! To have you greet me,
A man like you, after so long a time!
What brought you here, my son? What need impelled you
To anchor off this shore? What friendly wind?
Who are you? Tell me. Tell me everything.

NEOPTOLEMUS:

I am sailing to my island home, to Scyros.
My father was Achilles, and my name
Is Neoptolemus. Now you know all.

PHILOCTETES:

I loved your father well; I loved your country,   230
And your old foster-father, Lycomedes.
Why did you touch this coast? Where did you sail from?

NEOPTOLEMUS:

Well, since you ask me, I have sailed from Troy.

PHILOCTETES:

From Troy? How could you? You were not our shipmate
In the beginning when the fleet set out.

NEOPTOLEMUS:

Then you were with them on that expedition?

PHILOCTETES:

Can it be possible you do not know me?

NEOPTOLEMUS:

How could I know you when I never saw you?

PHILOCTETES:

You never heard my name? You heard no rumor
Of all the sufferings that have nearly killed me?   240

NEOPTOLEMUS:

No, nothing. Not a word of what you ask.

PHILOCTETES:

Oh, oh, what misery! How the gods must hate me!
To think that no one in my own home, no one
In all of Greece has learned about my fate.
Those impious men who cast me off and left me
Laugh and keep silent, while my sickness thrives,
Giving me greater torment. Oh, my boy,

Son of Achilles, I am Philoctetes,
The son of Poias. You may have heard of me
As master of the bow of Heracles.   250
The Cephallenian king and our two generals
Disgraced themselves by putting me ashore
Destitute, wasting away from a deadly wound,
The savage bite of a venomous adder. Son,
They left me here, left me with my infection
To keep me company. The fleet had sailed
From Chrysé to this coast. They were delighted
To see me sleeping, after a rough voyage,
Inside a rocky cave close by the sea.
There they abandoned me, leaving behind   260
A rag or two and a few bits of food.
May they come to that themselves! Think, my boy, think!
What an awakening when my sleep was over!
How my tears flowed, how my laments burst out!
For every ship was gone, all those I sailed with,
And there was no one left, no one to help me,
No one to ease the torment of my pain,
And searching everywhere I found no stock
Of anything but misery. Time went on,
Year after year, and in my small, cramped shelter   270
I had to meet my needs by my own efforts.
This bow appeased my hunger, bringing down
The swift-winged doves, and every time my arrows,
Sped by this bow-string, found their mark, I limped
Painfully to the spot, dragging along
My horrible foot. And then whenever water
Had to be brought or firewood broken up
During the winter frosts, I struggled out
And managed somehow, wretched as I am,
To do the work. And when I had no fire,   280
I would rub stones together till I kindled
The hidden spark. And so from day to day
I kept myself alive. Indeed, a roof
Over my head and fire give all I want
Except relief from pain. Son, let me tell you
What kind of place this island is. No sailor
Comes here by choice. There is no anchorage,
No town where he can sell his merchandise
Or find a welcome. No one in his senses
Has ever sailed here. Now and then, of course,   290
Some ship has put in of necessity.
In a long lifetime many things can happen.
These visitors, when they come, speak kindly to me

Or pity me enough, perhaps, to give me
Some food or a few clothes; but when I ask them,
There is one thing no one will do for me:
Take me home safely. I have been lingering here
Ten wretched years, hungry, in misery,
Feeding my ravenous infection. Son,
This is the way the Atridae and Odysseus   300
Have treated me. May the Olympian gods
Inflict on them the agony I have felt.

CHORUS:

I am as sorry for you, son of Poias,
As any of the others who have come here.

NEOPTOLEMUS:

And I can testify to what you said.
It is all true. For I have found Odysseus
And the Atridae villainous men to deal with.

PHILOCTETES:

What! Have the sons of Atreus made you suffer?
You have a score to settle with those scoundrels?

NEOPTOLEMUS:

If only I had power to slake my fury,   310
Then would both Sparta and Mycenae learn
That Scyros is the mother of brave men.

PHILOCTETES:

Well said, my son! You have come here hot with anger,
Railing against them. Why? What reason have you?

NEOPTOLEMUS:

It hurts to speak of it, but I will tell you
The wrong they did me when I came to Troy.
When destiny had decreed Achilles' death —

PHILOCTETES:

Wait! First of all let me be sure of this:
Achilles dead? Is that what you are saying?

NEOPTOLEMUS:

Yes. But a god and not a mortal killed him.   320
Apollo, men say, struck him with his arrow.

PHILOCTETES:

They were both great, the slayer and the slain.
Son, son! What shall I do first? Hear the story
Of your misfortune or lament for him?

NEOPTOLEMUS:

Sir, your own suffering is enough to weep for,
It seems to me, without regard for others.

PHILOCTETES:

Yes, that is very true. Well then, go on.
Tell me what happened. They insulted you?

NEOPTOLEMUS:

    Two of them came to get me in a ship
    Whose prow was bright with garlands: great Odysseus   330
    And Phoenix, the foster-father of Achilles.
    Their story, true or false, was this: that since
    My father was now dead, fate had decreed
    Troy should not fall except beneath my hand.
    When I heard that, I did not hesitate
    But sailed away at once, chiefly for love
    Of my dead father, whom I wished to see
    While he was still unburied. I had never
    Laid eyes on him. Besides, I was attracted
    By what they promised — if I went with them,   340
    I was to take the citadel of Troy.
    After a two-day voyage, rowing hard
    Before a favoring wind, we reached Sigéum,
    A hateful place. I had no sooner landed
    Than the whole army gathered round to give me
    A joyful welcome, vowing they saw Achilles
    Alive again. But he was lying dead.
    I wept for him, I, his ill-fated son.
    And then I went directly to the Atridae —
    My friends I thought — to claim my father's arms   350
    And everything else that he possessed. Their answer
    Was utterly shameless. How can I bear to tell you?
    "Son of Achilles, you are free to take
    All that your father left except his arms.
    Another man has those in his possession,
    Laertes' son." I leaped up, furious,
    With tear-filled eyes and cried out bitterly,
    "You scoundrels, have you dared to give my arms
    To someone else before you had my leave?"
    And then Odysseus spoke — he was close by: 360
    "Yes, boy. And they were right to give them to me.
    I saved them and the man they had belonged to."
    In a burst of rage, I called down on his head
    Curse after bitter curse — I spared him nothing —
    For carrying off my arms. This angered him,
    Though he was not quick-tempered, and he answered:
    "You were not with us here, you shirked your duty.
    And what is more, for all your insolent talk,
    You will never go back to Scyros with those arms."
    With that I sailed for home, taunted, insulted,   370
    Robbed of my own by that most evil son
    Of an evil race, Odysseus. Yet I think
    The kings are more to blame, because an army
    Is guided by its leaders, like a city.

Unruly men learn to do wrong from those
Who teach them wickedness. That is my story.
And may the man who hates the sons of Atreus
Be dear to all the gods as he is to me.

CHORUS:

Goddess of hills, of the golden sands of Pactólus,
    All-nourishing Earth, the mother of mighty Zeus,   380
We were there, dread Mother, the day when the two
    Atridae
    Heaped on our lord their insults and abuse.
When they gave Odysseus his father's matchless armor,
    We invoked thy name, we cried aloud in our need.
Thou bestriding the lions who slaughter the bulls and
    devour them,
      O goddess, give heed!

PHILOCTETES:

Strangers, you voyaged here with good credentials.
Your injury is the counterpart of mine,
Our stories are in tune. I recognize
The work of the Atridae and Odysseus,   390
For I know well he has a tongue prepared
To lend itself to any trick or falsehood
For some dishonest purpose. Nothing you say
Surprises me, except for the elder Ajax.
How could he stand there and endure the sight?

NEOPTOLEMUS:

He is dead, my friend. If he had been alive,
They would never have taken those arms away from me.

PHILOCTETES:

What did you say? Is he too dead and gone?

NEOPTOLEMUS:

Yes. Think of him as having left this light.

PHILOCTETES:

Dreadful! But Diomédes and Odysseus,   400
The son of Sísyphus bought by Laertes —
They will not die, for they ought not to live.

NEOPTOLEMUS:

No, they will not. You may be sure of that.
The army holds them both in high esteem.

PHILOCTETES:

But then, my good old friend, Nestor of Pylos,
Is he still living? He would keep in check
Their evil doing by his wise advice.

NEOPTOLEMUS:

Life has been hard for him. Antílochus,
His son who was at Troy with him, is dead.

PHILOCTETES:

What bitter news! You say two men are dead,   410
The two whose deaths I wanted least to hear of.
Ah! What can we expect to happen next?
Odysseus yet alive and those two gone!
He should be numbered with the dead, not they.

NEOPTOLEMUS:

He is a cunning wrestler, Philoctetes,
But even a clever man can be tripped up.

PHILOCTETES:

Where was Patróclus when you needed him,
Your father's dearest friend? Tell me, I beg you.

NEOPTOLEMUS:

He too was dead and gone. I tell you this:
War kills a worthless man only by chance   420
But never fails to single out a good one.

PHILOCTETES:

Yes, I agree with you. And there is someone
I want to know about, someone quite worthless.
Yet he is cunning and a clever speaker.

NEOPTOLEMUS:

The man you mean can only be Odysseus.

PHILOCTETES:

No, not Odysseus. He was called Thersítes,
Who talked repeatedly when no one wanted
To let him talk at all. Is he alive?

NEOPTOLEMUS:

I did not see him, but I heard he is.

PHILOCTETES:

He must be. Evil never yet has died.   430
The gods cherish it tenderly and take
A strange delight in turning back from Hades
Hardened, unscrupulous villains. Yet they always
Destroy the just and good. What can I think
About such things? How can I praise the gods,
When, in the act of praise, I find them evil?

NEOPTOLEMUS:

For my part, Philoctetes, in the future
I will be on my guard. I will be sure
To keep away from Troy and the Atridae.
A place in which the bad outweighs the good,   440
Where honor perishes and cowards rule,
Is not the place where I will make my friends.
No, from today I will be satisfied
With rocky Scyros. I ask nothing better
By way of home. Now I must board my ship.
Good-bye, then, Philoctetes. May the gods

Be good to you and give you the relief
You hope for from your suffering. Good-bye.
We must be off so as to lose no time
In sailing when the gods allow us to.   450

PHILOCTETES:
Son, are you starting now? NEOPTOLEMUS: Yes. The right
                place
To gauge the weather is beside the ship.

PHILOCTETES:
I beg you, in your father's name, your mother's,
In the name of everything that you hold dear
In your own home, I beg you not to leave me
Alone and helpless, wretched as you see me,
Wretched in ways I told you of. You need not
Make much of me. It will be difficult
With me on board as freight. That I know well.
But still, put up with me. To noble natures   460
Baseness is hateful, virtue glorious.
You will find yourself disgraced if you refuse me,
But if you help me, you will be crowned with honor
When I return alive to Oeta. Son!
Less than a day will see me off your hands.
Come! Make the effort. Do what you like with me.
Put me below deck, in the bow, the stern,
Wherever I will least disturb my shipmates.
Son, I implore you! Tell me you agree.
By mighty Zeus, the god of suppliants,   470
Here on my knees, a poor, maimed, feeble creature,
I beg you not to leave me destitute,
Far from the beaten path. No! Bring me back
Safely to your own home, or to Euboea,
The kingdom of Chalcódon. I would not
Have far to go from there to reach Mt. Oeta,
The heights of Trachis, and the full, swift flood
Of the Sperchéius. Then I could at last
See my dear father. I have been afraid
For years that he is dead. I sent him word   480
Time after time by those who passed this way,
Imploring him to have his own ship come
And bring me back. But either he has died,
Or else the messengers, as seems more likely,
Gave little thought to me and hurried home.
Now I have found escort and messenger,
For you are both. Have pity on me! Save me!
Men lead precarious lives — remember that —
Wavering between well-being and disaster.
A man in comfort should beware of danger   490

And keep sharp lookout when his life goes smoothly
Lest ruin strike before he is aware.

CHORUS:

Have pity, O King. He has suffered grievous hardship.
May no one I love undergo so much for so long!
Let him reap his reward, if you hate the wicked Atridae,
For they wronged him, those two, and you could re-
dress their wrong.
I would put him aboard your ship — it is swift and
well-fitted —
And carry him back to the home he yearns to see.
You avoid, O King, the risk of the gods' resentment
By granting his plea. 500

NEOPTOLEMUS:

Take care not to respond too readily.
When you are with him and you find his sickness
Hard to put up with, you may change your mind.

CHORUS:

No sir. I promise you will have no reason
Ever to blame me for a thing like that.

NEOPTOLEMUS:

It would be shameful if a stranger found me
Less prompt than you to help him in his need.
Let us set sail, if that is what you want.
Let the man come at once. Our ship will take him
Without objection. May the gods convey us 510
In safety to whatever port we sail for!

PHILOCTETES:

Oh, what a day! What happiness! If only
There were some way for me to prove my love
For you, my dearest friend, and your kind crew!
Let us be off when we have kissed the earth
Of my old home which was no home, that you
May learn how brave I was to keep alive.
After one look, I think, no other man
Could have endured it. Yet necessity
Has slowly taught me to put up with evil. 520

CHORUS:

Wait sirs. Two men are coming over there,
A shipmate and a stranger. Hear what it is
They have to say before you go inside.

Enter a sailor disguised as a MERCHANT
followed by another sailor

MERCHANT:

Son of Achilles, I asked this man to tell me
Where I could find you. There were three of them
On guard back at your ship. I meet you here

Quite unexpectedly, because I happened
To land on the same coast. I am the master
Of a small trader. I put out from Troy
And am now bound for home, Pepárethus,   530
The land of grapes. As soon as I discovered
Everyone here was in your crew, I thought
It wrong to sail away without a word,
For you could make it worth my while for me
To tell my news. Apparently you know
Nothing of your affairs, of the new plans
The Greeks have made for you. And they are not
Just planning, they are acting, acting quickly.

NEOPTOLEMUS:

Sir, I am grateful to you for your forethought.
Unless I prove base, I will not forget it.   540
But tell me what you mean. I want to know
The strange new plans you say the Greeks have made.

MERCHANT:

By now old Phoenix and the sons of Theseus
Have put to sea in full cry after you.

NEOPTOLEMUS:

To bring me back by force or by persuasion?

MERCHANT:

I do not know. I tell you what I heard.

NEOPTOLEMUS:

Can Phoenix and the others be so eager
To do this for the sake of the Atridae?

MERCHANT:

Well, they are doing it — not slowly either.

NEOPTOLEMUS:

Odysseus was not ready to set out   550
With his own message? Why? Was he afraid?

MERCHANT:

He and the son of Tydeus were in pursuit
Of someone else when I got under way.

NEOPTOLEMUS:

Who was it that Odysseus himself was after?

MERCHANT:

There was a man — But who is over there?
Tell me and keep your voice down when you speak.

NEOPTOLEMUS:

My friend, that is the famous Philoctetes.

MERCHANT:

Then ask me no more questions. Do not wait
A single moment longer. Leave at once.

PHILOCTETES:

What is it, son? Why is that sailor talking   560
In whispers with you, bargaining about me?

NEOPTOLEMUS:
>I do not know yet, but whatever it is,
>He must speak openly to all of us.

MERCHANT:
>Do not expose me. Do not tell the army
>I talk too much. I am a poor man, sir,
>And they are generous in their dealings with me.

NEOPTOLEMUS:
>I hate the sons of Atreus, and this man
>Is my best friend because he hates them too.
>If you have come here as a friend, you must not
>Keep from us anything that you may have heard.   570

MERCHANT:
>Be careful what you are doing. NEOPTOLEMUS: Yes, I have been.

MERCHANT:
>You must take the blame. NEOPTOLEMUS: By all means. Go
>   ahead.

MERCHANT:
>Well then, I will. This is the man those two
>Have sailed to get — the two I spoke about,
>The son of Tydeus and the great Odysseus.
>They swore a solemn oath they would persuade him
>Or force him to return. Beyond a doubt
>All the Achaeans heard the lord Odysseus
>When he said this, for of the two he had
>The greater confidence in his success.   580

NEOPTOLEMUS:
>After so long, what can have made the Atridae
>Feel such concern about a man like this,
>Someone they had abandoned years ago?
>This sudden yearning, was it the compulsion,
>The vengeance of the gods who punish evil?

MERCHANT:
>I will explain. Perhaps you have not heard.
>There was a man named Helenus, a prophet
>Of noble birth, one of the sons of Priam.
>Crafty Odysseus, who is always talked of
>In shameful terms, went out one night alone,   590
>Made him a prisoner, bound him up, and then
>Displayed his splendid prize before the Achaeans.
>Helenus prophesied of many things
>And in particular said this: that they
>Would never raze the citadel of Troy
>Unless they had persuaded Philoctetes
>To leave his island and return with them.
>Odysseus, when he heard that prophecy,
>Promised at once that he would get the man

And show him to the Greeks. Most probably   600
He would come willingly, but he would come
Willing or not. And then Odysseus added
That if he failed, they could cut off his head.
That is my news. And my advice to you
And any friend of yours is to leave quickly.

PHILOCTETES:

Awful! That monster promised to persuade me
To return to Troy? He might as well persuade me
To come from Hades to the light of day
After my death, the way his father came!

MERCHANT:

I have nothing to do with that. Well, I must go   610
Back to my ship. May the gods be good to you.

Exeunt MERCHANT *and* SAILOR

PHILOCTETES:

Son, it amazes me! How could Odysseus
Expect to tame me with his words, and lead me
Out of his ship, a spectacle for the Greeks?
He will never do it! I would rather hear
My deadliest enemy speak, the snake that left me
Without a foot. But there is nothing, nothing
He would not say or undertake. I know
That he will get here. Son, let us be off.
Let us make sure a wide sea lies between   620
Odysseus' ship and ours. Come, come away!
The utmost effort at the critical moment
Brings rest and slumber when the task is done.

NEOPTOLEMUS:

Then we will sail as soon as the head wind drops.
Just now, however, it is dead against us.

PHILOCTETES:

All winds are fair when you escape from evil.

NEOPTOLEMUS:

Yes, but this weather is against *them* too.

PHILOCTETES:

Weather can never be against a pirate,
When he is setting out to rob and plunder.

NEOPTOLEMUS:

Well, if you wish to go, then we will go.   630
Bring what you need or what you want the most.

PHILOCTETES:

I need some things, but I have little choice.

NEOPTOLEMUS:

What is there that my ship cannot supply?

PHILOCTETES:
> I always keep a certain herb with me
> To soothe my pain. It gives me great relief.

NEOPTOLEMUS:
> Get that then, and what else you want to take.

PHILOCTETES:
> I may have dropped some arrows and overlooked them.
> I cannot leave them here to be picked up.

NEOPTOLEMUS:
> Is that the famous bow, then, which you have there?

PHILOCTETES:
> This is the one, this bow here in my hand.   640

NEOPTOLEMUS:
> Am I allowed to look at it more closely,
> Hold it, and honor it as a holy thing?

PHILOCTETES:
> Yes, son, you are allowed to. You may have it
> And anything else of mine that you can use.

NEOPTOLEMUS:
> I certainly long to hold it, if I have
> A right to. But if not, then never mind.

PHILOCTETES:
> You are reverent, my son. Your wish is lawful.
> You, you alone have let me see the daylight,
> My friends, the land of Oeta, my old father.
> When I was prostrate at my enemies' feet,   650
> You raised me up beyond their reach. Fear nothing.
> Here. You may take the bow and give it back.
> Then you can boast that to reward your goodness
> You were the only man who ever touched it.
> I too was given it for a kindly act.

NEOPTOLEMUS:
> I am glad I found you, glad I won your friendship.
> A man's most prized possession is a friend
> Who can repay one benefit by another.
> Go in, sir. PHILOCTETES: Yes. And I will take you too.
> Sick as I am I need to have you with me.   660

> *Exeunt* NEOPTOLEMUS *and* PHILOCTETES

CHORUS:
> I have not seen the man who sought to dishonor
> > The bed of Zeus in the days of old
> And was bound to a rolling wheel by the son of Cronos;
> > I have heard his story told.
> But no one else have I seen or heard of who suffered
> > Like Philoctetes. He was kind and fair
> In all his dealings, yet how hard, how cruel
> > Was the fate he had to bear,

Hearing the beat of the sea as it broke around him
    For all these solitary years.   670
I marvel how he has kept his hold unshaken
    On a life so steeped in tears.

Unable to walk he had no one in all the island
    To hear his laments or heed the cries
Wrung from his lips by the plague that drained and
           consumed him,
    No one to sympathize
Or find a way of ministering to his comfort
    By gleaning from the earth's abundant store
Some herb that would bring relief to the burning anguish
    Of his foot's oozing sore.   680
Then like a child without a nurse to tend him,
    He would drag himself here and there in quest
Of means to support his life, whenever his torment
           Gave him a moment's rest.

    The holy earth's life-giving harvests,
All the food that rewards our mortal toil he was forced to
           forgo,
    With nothing to stay his pangs of hunger
Except what his winged arrows now and again brought low;
    With never a cup of wine to cheer him,
And for all his constant seeking, nothing to quench his
           thirst   690
    Save at times a pool of stagnant water.
Poor wretch! For ten bitter years he has led a life accursed.
      PHILOCTETES *and* NEOPTOLEMUS *are seen entering*

    But now he has done with all these evils;
For happiness lies ahead, and greatness at last is in store.
    Swift is his path across the ocean,
For this son of a noble house is bringing him home once more,
    Home to the banks of the Spercheius,
To the haunt of the Malian nymphs, where above Mt.
           Oeta's height
    The lord of the brazen shield ascended
In glory to the gods as the holy fire burned bright.   700
NEOPTOLEMUS:
    Come, sir, with me. Why are you standing there
    Without a word to say? Are you struck dumb?
PHILOCTETES (*crying out*):
    Oh! Oh!
NEOPTOLEMUS:
    What is the matter? PHILOCTETES: Nothing, son. Go on.

NEOPTOLEMUS:
Is it your old wound? Are you still in pain?
PHILOCTETES:
No. I am better for the moment. Gods!
NEOPTOLEMUS:
Why do you call on the gods with such a groan?
PHILOCTETES:
To ask them to be kind, to come and save us.
Oh! Oh!
NEOPTOLEMUS:
What is it? Let me know. Do not persist   710
In keeping silent. There must be something wrong.
PHILOCTETES:
It is destroying me. I can no longer
Hide it from you. Oh! Oh! It pierces me,
Pierces me through and through. What agony!
I am eaten up with torture. Oh! Oh! Son,
If you have a sword, I beg you by the gods
Take it and cut my heel off, cut it off!
Do not spare my life. Be quick, son! Oh, be quick!
NEOPTOLEMUS:
What is it now? What can have happened to you?
Why do you suddenly shriek and groan that way?   720
PHILOCTETES:
You know. NEOPTOLEMUS: What is the matter? PHILOCTETES:
Son, you know.
NEOPTOLEMUS:
What do you mean? PHILOCTETES: You *must* know, son. Oh!
Oh!
NEOPTOLEMUS:
Your sickness is a terrible load to bear.
PHILOCTETES:
Beyond words terrible. Have pity on me!
NEOPTOLEMUS:
What shall I do? PHILOCTETES: Do not abandon me.
Do not be frightened. My tormentor comes
Only from time to time, perhaps when tired
Of wandering elsewhere. NEOPTOLEMUS: Ah! I pity you.
There is nothing, nothing that you have not suffered.
How can I help? Would you like to have me hold you?   730
PHILOCTETES:
No, no, not that! But take this bow of mine —
Just now you asked for it — until the pain
That is convulsing me has died away.
Guard it well. Keep it safe. As the attack
Wears off, I fall asleep, and then the torture
At last will stop. But you must let me sleep

Without disturbance. Meanwhile if they come,
By all the gods I beg you not to let them
Persuade or force you to give up the bow.
Otherwise you will bring destruction down   740
On your own head and mine, your suppliant's.

NEOPTOLEMUS:

    I shall take care. You may be sure of that.
No one except ourselves shall ever touch it.
Give me the bow, and may good luck come with it.

PHILOCTETES:

    There. Take it, son. Reverence the jealous gods.
Pray that it may not bring on you the evils
It brought on me and on its earlier master.

NEOPTOLEMUS:

    You gods, grant us this prayer. Grant us fair winds
And a swift voyage to whatever port
You sanction for us and we have in mind.   750

PHILOCTETES:

    I am afraid, son, that your prayer is useless.
Look there. Dark clots of blood are oozing up
Out of the wound. And there is worse to follow,
More torment from this cursed foot of mine.
It is coming, coming! Now you understand!
Oh! Oh! How fearful! Stay here, stay with me!
If only *you* might feel this pain, Odysseus,
Piercing you to the heart. Oh! Oh! Again!
And you two, Agamemnon, Menelaus,
You generals, if only you might suffer   760
As I have suffered, and as long. Death! Death!
Day after day I have been calling you.
Why can you never come? Son, you are kind.
Take me. Consume me in the fire of Lemnos.
I myself did that for the son of Zeus,
Knowing I acted rightly, and was given
As a reward those arms now in your keeping.
What is your answer, son? What is your answer?
Why are you silent? What has happened to you?

NEOPTOLEMUS:

    It wrings my heart to see you in such pain.   770

PHILOCTETES:

    Do not be too concerned. Sharp as it is,
The pain goes quickly. But I beg you, son,
I beg you not to leave me here alone.

NEOPTOLEMUS:

    You need fear nothing. PHILOCTETES: You will stay?
        NEOPTOLEMUS: Of course.

141

PHILOCTETES:
Well, I ought not to ask you for your oath.
NEOPTOLEMUS:
It is my duty not to go without you.
PHILOCTETES:
Give me your hand on that. NEOPTOLEMUS: There. I will stay.
PHILOCTETES:
Now, take me off. NEOPTOLEMUS: What do you mean?
PHILOCTETES: Up there.
NEOPTOLEMUS:
What madness makes you look up to the sky?
PHILOCTETES:
Oh! Let me go. NEOPTOLEMUS: Where? PHILOCTETES: Let me
go, I tell you. 780
NEOPTOLEMUS:
No, I will not. PHILOCTETES: You kill me when you touch me.
NEOPTOLEMUS:
Then I will let you go. You are calmer now.
PHILOCTETES:
Be gentle, earth. I am about to die.
This agony is too great. I cannot stand.
NEOPTOLEMUS:
In a few minutes more he will be sleeping,
It seems to me. His head has fallen backward,
His body is soaked in sweat from head to foot,
And from his heel the thick blood gushes out
In a dark stream. Come, let us leave him, friends.
Let him lie quietly till he falls asleep. 790
CHORUS:
O kindly sleep, that knows no suffering,
Come gently down to him and gently spread
Your cloud of radiance above his head.
Hear us O Lord of healing! Hear O King!
What will you do now, son? What have you planned?
Why are we waiting? We should not be slow,
For chance, when the right moment is at hand,
Wins many triumphs at a single blow.
NEOPTOLEMUS:
I know he can hear nothing, but I know
It is in vain that we possess the bow. 800
We cannot leave him here. His is to be
The crown of victory by the gods' decree.
We would degrade ourselves in all men's eyes
Boasting we basely won a useless prize.
CHORUS:
My son, some god will see to that. Speak low.
Whisper your answer, because all men sleep

Lightly when they are suffering and keep
Their eyes and ears on guard. Let him not know.
Exert yourself to do it while you can
Before he wakes. In what *you* mean to do   810
  If you persist in it, a prudent man
Can see the endless ills that will ensue.

    Now, son, the wind is fair. There on the ground
He lies in darkness, sightless, without defense,
  For in the hot sun sleep is sound.
Handless, footless, bereft of every sense,
  He lies as if stretched out dead.
Think of your plan. Consider. Is it wise
When everything hangs in the balance? In our eyes
  That act is best which causes the least dread.   820

NEOPTOLEMUS:

Be quiet, I tell you. Keep your wits about you.
His eyes are opening. Look. He lifts his head.

PHILOCTETES:

Ah, sunlight after sleep, and friends to guard me!
How could I dream of anything like that?
How could I dare to hope you would have the patience
To stay beside me here, take pity on me,
Bear with me, help relieve my pain? The Atridae,
Those great commanders, certainly did not show
Any such readiness to assume that burden.
But you have a noble nature and were born   830
Of noble parents. You have disregarded
Everything that repelled you, my loud cries
And this offensive smell. And for a time
I can forget my pain and rest a little.
Come here, son. Lift me, put me on my feet.
Then when my faintness leaves me, we can go
Down to the ship and put to sea at once.

NEOPTOLEMUS:

This is a welcome sight I never hoped for.
You are alive, awake, and free from torment.
With all the agonies you had endured   840
You seemed on the point of death. Now then stand up.
Or if you would rather, I will have these men
Carry you. They will gladly undertake
That task, since you and I are of one mind.

PHILOCTETES:

Thank you, son. Help me as you said you would,
You, not your men. I do not want them troubled
By this foul smell of mine before they need be.
It will be hard enough with me on board.

NEOPTOLEMUS:
Just as you like. There sir, take hold yourself.

PHILOCTETES:
You need not worry. Habit will get me up.   850

NEOPTOLEMUS:
I cannot endure it! What am I to do?

PHILOCTETES:
What is it, son? What do you mean by that?

NEOPTOLEMUS:
How can I tell you? Where can I find the words?

PHILOCTETES:
Find words for what? Son, do not talk that way.

NEOPTOLEMUS:
As matters stand, I do not know what to say.

PHILOCTETES:
You cannot take me? Did you change your mind
Because you could not bear my loathsome sickness?

NEOPTOLEMUS:
There is nothing that is not loathsome when a man
Corrupts his nature by the things he does.

PHILOCTETES:
But you are faithful to your father's nature   860
When you help someone who deserves your help.

NEOPTOLEMUS:
I will seem unprincipled. The thought is torture.

PHILOCTETES:
You have been true, but what you say is frightening.

NEOPTOLEMUS:
What shall I do? Zeus! Shall I twice prove false
By shameful silence and by shameful speech?

PHILOCTETES:
Unless I am mistaken this man means
To break his faith, forsake me, and sail off.

NEOPTOLEMUS:
No, not forsake you, but take you on a voyage
That will prove bitter, and I dread the thought.

PHILOCTETES:
What do you mean? I do not understand.   870

NEOPTOLEMUS:
I will hide nothing. You must sail for Troy,
To the Achaeans, the Atridae's army.

PHILOCTETES:
Oh no! NEOPTOLEMUS: Wait. Do not groan before you learn —

PHILOCTETES:
Learn what? What are you going to do with me?

NEOPTOLEMUS:
First, rescue you from all this misery,
And then lay waste the plains of Troy with you.

144

PHILOCTETES:
    You mean that? You are certain? NEOPTOLEMUS: Yes. I must
    Of harsh necessity. Do not be angry.
PHILOCTETES:
    I am lost, betrayed! What have you done to me?
    Give me my bow back, stranger. Now. At once.   880
NEOPTOLEMUS:
    I cannot do it. I must obey my leaders.
    Duty compels me and my own self-interest.
PHILOCTETES:
    You fiend, you absolute monster, you past master
    Of horrible trickery! How could you do this,
    Deceive me this way? Are you not ashamed
    To look at me, who knelt down at your feet
    Begging for pity? How could you be so cruel?
    You killed me when you took away my bow.
    Give it back to me! Son, give it back to me,
    I beg you, I beseech you! By the gods   890
    Of your fathers, do not rob me of my life!
    Dreadful! he does not speak. He looks away.
    He will not give it up. You bays and headlands,
    You creatures of the hills with whom I live,
    You rugged crags, all of you old companions,
    To you I cry. Who else is there to listen?
    Hear how Achilles' son has treated me.
    He promised me that he would take me home;
    He takes me off to Troy. He pledged his word
    With his right hand in mine, and he has seized   900
    The bow of Heracles the son of Zeus,
    My sacred bow, and means to show his prize
    To all the Argives. He is dragging me
    Away with him as though he had taken prisoner
    Some mighty champion. He cannot see
    That he is killing a corpse, a shade, a vapor,
    The merest phantom. If I had had my strength,
    He would never have captured me, and even now
    He had to cheat me. I am betrayed, destroyed!
    What can I do now? Give me back the bow.   910
    Be your true self again. Say that you will.
    What! Silent? Then there is no hope for me.
    Once more I must return to those two doors
    Up in the rocks, stripped of my arms, unable
    To keep alive. Yes, I shall waste away
    There in that cave alone. No soaring bird,
    No beast that roams the mountains will that bow
    Of mine bring down. No, I myself, poor wretch,
    Shall make a feast for those on whom I fed,
    The quarry of those I hunted. I shall give   920

My life's blood to requite the blood I shed,
Because it seemed this man here knew no evil.
Die, curse you! No. Perhaps you will change your mind.
If not, then may you meet a frightful end!

CHORUS:
What shall we do, sir? Shall we sail away
Or give him what he asks? You must decide.

NEOPTOLEMUS:
Compassion for the man has wrung my heart,
Not now for the first time but long ago.

PHILOCTETES:
Show mercy, son! Do not expose yourself
To insult and abuse for tricking me.   930

NEOPTOLEMUS:
What shall I do? Why did I leave my home
To find myself in such a strait as this?

PHILOCTETES:
You are not wicked. I think you were taught your part
By wicked men. It suits them. Let them play it.
But as for you, give me my arms and go.

ODYSSEUS *enters behind with two sailors*

NEOPTOLEMUS:
What shall we do, men? ODYSSEUS: What is going on?
Stand back, you scoundrel! Let me have the bow.

PHILOCTETES:
Who can that be? What! Do I hear Odysseus?

ODYSSEUS:
Yes, you are right. Odysseus. Here before you.

PHILOCTETES:
This is the end of me! He was the man   940
Who captured me and robbed me of my arms.

ODYSSEUS:
Yes I, and no one else. That I admit.

PHILOCTETES:
Give me the bow, son. Give it back. ODYSSEUS: No, never.
Not even if he wished to. What is more
You must come with it or be forced to come.

PHILOCTETES:
What villainy! What matchless insolence!
Force me to come? ODYSSEUS: Unless you are willing to.

PHILOCTETES:
O land of Lemnos and all conquering flame,
You that Hephaestus kindled, must I bear it?
Must that man be allowed to drag me off?   950

ODYSSEUS:
I tell you it is Zeus who rules this country.
This is the will of Zeus. I am his servant.

PHILOCTETES:

    Scoundrel, what lies you can invent! You plead
    The sanction of the gods and make them liars.

ODYSSEUS:

    No. They are truthful. We must start our journey.

PHILOCTETES:

    Never. ODYSSEUS: I say you shall. You must obey me.

PHILOCTETES:

    How miserable a fate! I am not free.
    It is clear that I was born to be a slave.

ODYSSEUS:

    No slave. The equal of the greatest heroes.
    With them you will bring down Troy in utter ruin.   960

PHILOCTETES:

    No, no, not that. I will endure the worst
    Rather than that. This island has steep cliffs.

ODYSSEUS:

    What do you mean to do? PHILOCTETES: Throw myself **down**
    And dash my brains out on the rocks below.

ODYSSEUS (*to his men*):

    Hold him, you two. Keep him from doing it.

PHILOCTETES:

    Poor hands, the prey that man has bound together,
    Useless without the weapons that you love!
    (*to* ODYSSEUS) You have never had an honest, generous thought.
    You have pursued me, stalked me, hiding behind a boy
    I did not know. He is too good for you,   970
    My kind of boy, whose one concern has been
    To obey his orders. Already it is clear
    He bitterly regrets his own mistakes
    And the pain he brought on me. But your vile soul,
    Peering from ambush as it always is,
    Taught him by slow degrees the art of evil,
    Unfitted and unwilling though he was.
    Now you intend to truss me up—how shameful! —
    And carry me from the shore on which you flung me,
    Helpless, friendless, without a city, dead   980
    Among the living. Curse you! That has been
    My frequent prayer. But since the gods grant nothing
    To comfort me, you are alive and happy.
    For me life is all pain, steeped as I am
    In misery and laughed at both by you
    And by the two Atridae, the commanders
    Whom you obey. And yet they had to trick you
    To get their yoke on you and make you sail.
    But as for me, poor creature that I am,
    I sailed of my own accord with seven ships   990
    To be disgraced, cast out, by them you tell me,

By you they say. Why do you drag me off?
What will you gain? I can mean nothing to you.
I have long been dead. You whom the gods detest,
How does it happen you no longer find me
Maimed and foul smelling? Once I have sailed with you,
How can you offer your burnt sacrifices?
How can you pour drink offerings to the gods?
That was your pretext when you banished me.
May you die a dreadful death! And die you shall   1000
For the wrong you have done me, if the gods love justice.
But I am sure they do, for you would never
Have sailed to seek a man so miserable
Unless the gods had goaded you into action.
Land of my fathers! Ever watchful gods!
If you can pity me, take vengeance, vengeance
At long last on them all. Truly my lot
Is pitiable, but if I saw their ruin,
I could believe my sickness at an end.

CHORUS:

The man is bitter, and his words are bitter.   1010
He does not yield to suffering, Odysseus.

ODYSSEUS:

If time served, I could answer him at length,
But as things are, I will say only this:
I am whatever man the occasion calls for.
When justice and nobility are at stake,
No one is more punctilious than I.
I am always out for victory, however,
Except this once. Now I will readily
Give way to you. Release him. Do not touch him.
Let him stay here. We have no use for you   1020
Now that we have your arms. Teucer is with us,
Who has the skill to use them, and I think
That I can master them as well as you,
And aim with as true a hand. Why do we need you?
Pace all of Lemnos. You are welcome to it.
We must be leaving. And perhaps your prize
Will bring to me the fame you should have won.

PHILOCTETES:

Oh, oh, how awful! What! Will you appear
Among the Argives decked out in my arms?

ODYSSEUS:

No more. No further talking. I am going.   1030

PHILOCTETES:

Son of Achilles, will you speak to me?
Or will you also leave without a word?

ODYSSEUS:

    Come. Do not even look at him, for fear
    Your nobleness may ruin our good fortune.

PHILOCTETES (*to* CHORUS):

    And you, my friends, will you too leave me here
    Alone and helpless? Will you show no pity?

CHORUS:

    There is our captain, that young man. Whatever
    Answer he makes must be our answer also.

NEOPTOLEMUS:

    I will be called too sympathetic. Still,
    Stay here with Philoctetes, if he wants you.   1040
    Wait till the crew have finished making ready
    To put to sea, and we have prayed to the gods.
    By then, perhaps, he may think better of us.
    We two will go now. When we send for you,
    You are to come to us without delay.

                  Exeunt ODYSSEUS *and* NEOPTOLEMUS

PHILOCTETES:

    O cavern, now icy cold, now hot!
      O rocky cave!
    I have been fated never to leave this spot.
      Here is my destined grave.
    Unhappy dwelling haunted by my pain,   1050
    What hope is left me, now that I remain?
      How can I keep alive? For I must lie
        Abandoned, ill-bestead,
    Watching the timorous doves in the shrill wind fly
      Unharmed above my head.

CH.:   Poor wretch, this is your doing, yours alone.
      No force outside yourself can be accused.
    With two ways open, wisdom you might have shown.
      You chose the evil and the good refused.

PHILOCTETES:

    Broken, broken with agony,   1060
      Here must I stay.
    With no one beside me, no one to comfort me
      Here must I waste away,
    Taking no food home that my swift-winged bow,
    Held steadily in my strong hands, brought low.
      Deceit and treachery caught me in their snare.
      And the man who did this wrong,
    May he feel as keenly the pangs I have had to bear,
      And feel them for as long.

CH.: The gods have fated you to suffer thus.   1070
In no deceit have we played any part.
Let not your fearful curses fall on us.
Friendship with you is very near our heart.

PHILOCTETES:
How can I bear it? Well I know
There where the white wave breaks upon the shore,
He sits and mocks me, brandishing my bow,
The bow no other living man has borne
Ever before.
My treasure, my deliverer, now torn
From the hands that loved you, torn away,   1080
If you were human, you would pity me,
Heracles' friend you will no longer see.
A new and cunning master you obey.
Now you must undergo
His wickedness, and learn the vile pretense,
The evil stratagems my hated foe
Has practiced countless times at my expense.
CH.: A man is just when he the truth defends,
Not when he lets abuse get out of hand.
Odysseus did good service for his friends   1090
As the army's envoy, coming at its command.

PHILOCTETES:
Swift birds, whom I shot down in flight,
Fierce, bright-eyed mountain creatures, from whose lairs
I made you start up, flee not from my sight.
The arms that in times past have made me strong
Another bears.
Oh! I am lost, the victim of bitter wrong!
The land is yours now. Range at will.
From this time forward you need fear no more.
My blood for your blood — there is ample store   1100
Of my corrupted flesh. Come. Eat your fill,
My body for your own.
I shall be dead soon. How is a man to live
Without resources? On the wind alone,
Powerless to capture what the earth can give?
CH.: We came in kindness. Do not turn away.
You can escape your lot, whose cruel pain
Feeds on your body, leaving you the prey
Of countless ills that follow in its train.

PHILOCTETES:
Once more, once more you put me on the rack,   1110
Though you are kind, the kindest of all who have come here.

150

Why have you done this? Why do you hurt me so?

CH.: What do you mean? PHILOCTETES: To carry me back
To the Troy I hate — that was the thing you hoped for.

CH.: We thought it best. PHILOCTETES: Then leave me. Go.

CH.: Just as you wish. We obey that order with pleasure.
Be off to the ship, men. On your way.

PHIL.: Wait! In the name of Zeus who hears men's curses!

CH.: Steady, sir. PHILOCTETES: Friends, by the gods I beg you! Stay!

CH.: Why do you ask? PHILOCTETES: Oh! My fate! How, how can
I bear it?   1120
What can I do?
My foot! My foot! What will happen? Friends, come back
here!

CH.: You told us to go. Are we now to do something new?

PHIL.: I was convulsed with pain. You should not be angry
At the way I spoke when I was out of my mind.

CH.: Poor man, then come with us as we are asking.

PHIL.: No! Never! Not if I were to find
The lord of lightning himself about to consume me
With the blazing fire of his bolts. Let Ilium fall!
And let them perish by Ilium's wall,   1130
The men who could cast me away, a cripple!
I ask one thing of you, friends. Be kind.

CH.: What do you want? PHILOCTETES: A sword, if you have one,
An axe, any weapon.

CH.: What rashness have you in mind?

PHIL.: I would chop my body in pieces, hack myself limb from limb!
Death, death is all I can think of.

CH.: Why is that? PHILOCTETES: To find my father, to go to him.

CH.: Where? PHILOCTETES: In Hades. No more in the sun.
O city! O land of my fathers! Would I could see you!   1140
Fool that I was to have left your sacred river
To help my enemies, the Argives!
I am undone, undone.

CHORUS:
I would have left you a long time ago
And started for the ship, except for seeing
Odysseus coming and Achilles' son.

> *Exit* PHILOCTETES *into the cave*
> *Enter* ODYSSEUS *and* NEOPTOLEMUS

ODYSSEUS:
Why have you hurried back here? Will you tell me?

NEOPTOLEMUS:
I did wrong. I have come to set it right.

ODYSSEUS:
You talk in riddles. Wrong? What have you done?

NEOPTOLEMUS:
> I have obeyed your orders and the army's. 1150
ODYSSEUS:
> What you did then had nothing wrong about it.
NEOPTOLEMUS:
> I tricked a man, deceived him shamefully.
ODYSSEUS:
> What man? What will you do? Not something reckless?
NEOPTOLEMUS:
> No, nothing reckless. But to Philoctetes —
ODYSSEUS:
> And what of him? I feel a strange misgiving.
NEOPTOLEMUS:
> I took away his bow and I intend —
ODYSSEUS:
> Zeus! Are you saying you will give it back?
NEOPTOLEMUS:
> I say just that. I have no right to it.
ODYSSEUS:
> By all the gods! Can you be joking with me?
NEOPTOLEMUS:
> Yes, if to speak the truth can be called joking. 1160
ODYSSEUS:
> Son of Achilles, tell me what you mean.
NEOPTOLEMUS:
> How often must I tell you? Twice? Three times?
ODYSSEUS:
> I had no desire to hear you even once.
NEOPTOLEMUS:
> Then certainly I have nothing more to say.
ODYSSEUS:
> You can be stopped. There is a power to stop you.
NEOPTOLEMUS:
> What do you mean? Who is it? Who will stop me?
ODYSSEUS:
> The whole Greek army, I myself among them.
NEOPTOLEMUS:
> You are a wise man — talking utter nonsense.
ODYSSEUS:
> And what you do as well as say is nonsense.
NEOPTOLEMUS:
> Yet is it better to be just than wise. 1170
ODYSSEUS:
> How is it just to give up what you won
> By my advice? NEOPTOLEMUS: I have disgraced myself.
> I must try to make amends for my wrongdoing.
ODYSSEUS:
> You do not fear the Greeks in doing this?

NEOPTOLEMUS:

    With justice on my side, no threat you make
    Can give me pause, nor will I yield to force.

ODYSSEUS:

    Then we shall fight with *you*, not with the Trojans.

NEOPTOLEMUS:

    Very well then, we shall fight. ODYESSUS: Do you see my hand
    Reach for my sword? NEOPTOLEMUS: And you can see my hand
    Doing the same, and doing it at once.   1180

ODYSSEUS:

    No. I will let you alone. I will go back
    And tell the army. They will punish you.

NEOPTOLEMUS:

    How very sensible! Keep on like that
    And you will probably stay out of trouble.

                       Exit ODYSSEUS

    Come, Philoctetes! I am calling you
    Come. Leave that home of yours up in the rocks.

PHILOCTETES (*within*):

    What is that noise out there? Is someone calling?
    Why should you get me out? What do you want?

                    Enter PHILOCTETES

    Here is an ominous sight. Can you have come
    With some new torment after all the others?   1190

NEOPTOLEMUS:

    You need fear nothing. Only listen to me.

PHILOCTETES:

    You frighten me. I listened to you once,
    And your fine speeches brought disaster on me.

NEOPTOLEMUS:

    Do you think repentance is impossible?

PHILOCTETES:

    You talked the same way when you stole my bow.
    Your hidden treachery inspired my trust.

NEOPTOLEMUS:

    I am not treacherous now. I want to know
    Whether you will insist on staying here
    Or sail away with us. PHILOCTETES: No more. No more.
    Whatever you say will be a waste of time.   1200

NEOPTOLEMUS:

    You are sure of this? PHILOCTETES: Surer than words can tell.

NEOPTOLEMUS:

    I hoped that I could make you listen to me,
    But this is not the moment to persuade you.
    I have nothing more to say. PHILOCTETES: It would be useless.
    Make me your friend? No, you could never do it,
    You who deceived me, robbed me of my life,

And then came back to give me your advice,
The hateful son of a most noble father.
If only all of you were dead, the Atridae,
Laertes' son, and you! NEOPTOLEMUS: Stop. No more
   curses.   1210
Come take it. I am giving you your bow.

PHILOCTETES:
What did you say? Is this another trick?

NEOPTOLEMUS:
No, by the sacred majesty of Zeus.

PHILOCTETES:
O welcome words, if they can be believed!

NEOPTOLEMUS:
The act will prove them true. Stretch out your hand.
Make yourself master of your bow again.
       Enter ODYSSEUS *behind*

ODYSSEUS:
He shall not! May the gods be witnesses.
I speak for the Atridae and the army.

PHILOCTETES:
Whose voice was that, son? Did I hear Odysseus?

ODYSSEUS:
You did. And you can see him here beside you. 1220
I intend to drag you off with me to Troy
With or without Achilles' son's consent.

PHILOCTETES:
You will pay dearly if my aim is true.

NEOPTOLEMUS:
No! Do not shoot. I beg you by the gods.

PHILOCTETES:
Let me alone! Dear son, let me alone!

NEOPTOLEMUS:
I cannot do it.
       Exit ODYSSEUS

PHIL.:   Why did you hold me back
When I could have killed my hated enemy?

NEOPTOLEMUS:
Because we would be dishonored, both of us.

PHILOCTETES:
Well, there is one thing obvious. These princes, 1230
These lying heralds of the Achaean army,
Though brave in words are cowards in a fight.

NEOPTOLEMUS:
Yes. And you have your bow. Now you can find
No reason to be angry or reproach me.

PHILOCTETES:

    No. None. You show the qualities of the house
    From which you come, no child of Sisyphus
    But of Achilles, peerless when he was living
    As he is peerless now among the dead.

NEOPTOLEMUS:

    The praise you give my father and give me
    Is good to hear. But now I am going to ask   1240
    A favor of you. Men must endure the fates
    The gods impose on them, but those who cling
    To misery voluntarily, as you do,
    Cannot in justice be excused or pitied.
    You have become a savage. You refuse
    To listen to anyone. Even a friend
    Who gives you his advice from pure good will
    You think a deadly enemy, and hate him.
    Still, I intend to speak, and call on Zeus,
    Who hears the oaths of men, to be my witness.   1250
    Mark my words well and write them in your heart.
    The gods allotted you the pain you suffer
    Because you came upon the hidden serpent
    That guarded Chrysé's roofless sanctuary.
    Nor will you be relieved of your affliction,
    You may be certain, while the sun still rises
    And sets as it does now, till you are willing
    To come to Troy. There you will find with us
    The two sons of Asclépius, who will heal you.
    Then with your bow, and with the help I give you,   1260
    You will bring down the walls of Troy in ruin.
    I know this will take place because we captured
    A Trojan prisoner named Helenus,
    A famous prophet, and he told us plainly
    That all these happenings had been decreed,
    And furthermore that Troy was doomed to fall
    This present summer. If his words proved false,
    He said that we could have him put to death.
    Now that you know, give way with a good grace.
    Think of how greatly you will benefit.   1270
    You will be tended by skilled hands and healed.
    You will be called the bravest of the Greeks.
    You will win matchless fame by taking Troy,
    The city that has caused so many tears.

PHILOCTETES:

    My life is hateful. Why must I see the light
    Instead of going down to join the dead?
    What shall I do? How can I doubt the truth
    Of what he says, when the advice he gives

Is kindly meant? Then shall I yield to him?
In that case, how can I expose myself   1280
To public view, as wretched as I am?
Will anyone speak to me? These eyes of mine
Have witnessed everything that I have suffered.
Can they endure to see me face to face
With the two sons of Atreus who destroyed me,
Or with Laertes' evil-minded son?
I am not stung with anger for the past,
But I foresee the pain they will inflict
In days to come, for when the mind has once
Conceived and brought forth evil, it will teach   1290
Men to be evil always. As for you,
I wonder at the part you played. You never
Should have set out for Troy, and should have stopped
My going there. They held you in contempt
By robbing you of your father's arms, the gift
That he was honored with. Do you intend
To fight their battle, and make me fight as well?
No son, not that. You swore you would take me home.
Now keep your oath, and then go home yourself
And stay in Scyros. Let those evil men   1300
Come to their evil end. Then I shall have
Two things to thank you for, as will my father,
And you can save yourself from being thought
As wicked as the wickedness you helped.

NEOPTOLEMUS:
    You are persuasive. Still, I beg of you
    To trust the gods and trust what I have said.
    Accept my friendship and sail off with me.

PHILOCTETES:
    What! Go to Troy and to the man I hate,
    The son of Atreus, with this frightful foot?

NEOPTOLEMUS:
    No. But to those who can relieve your pain   1310
    And find a remedy for your ulcered leg.

PHILOCTETES:
    Do you mean those terrible things that you are saying?

NEOPTOLEMUS:
    I see what would be best for both of us.

PHILOCTETES:
    The gods can hear you. Do you feel no shame?

NEOPTOLEMUS:
    Why should it shame a man to help his friends?

PHILOCTETES:
    Do you mean to help me or the sons of Atreus?

NEOPTOLEMUS:
    You. Certainly I speak as friend to friend.

PHILOCTETES:
>   When you would put me in my enemies' power?

NEOPTOLEMUS:
>   You should learn to be less stubborn in misfortune.

PHILOCTETES:
>   I know you will be my ruin with your urging.   1320

NEOPTOLEMUS:
>   Not I. You do not understand, I tell you.

PHILOCTETES:
>   I understand the Atridae cast me off.

NEOPTOLEMUS:
>   But now they will restore your life to you.

PHILOCTETES:
>   Not if I must consent to go to Troy.

NEOPTOLEMUS:
>   Then what am I to do? I cannot hope
>   To win you over. It would be easiest
>   For me to say no more and let you live,
>   As you are living now, past hope of rescue.

PHILOCTETES:
>   Let me endure the pain that is my lot.
>   You put your hand in mine and promised me   1330
>   That you would take me home. Son, keep your promise.
>   Keep it at once, and do not speak of Troy,
>   For I have had my fill of lamentation.

NEOPTOLEMUS (*after a pause*):
>   Then since you want to, come. PHILOCTETES: Ah! Nobly spoken!

NEOPTOLEMUS:
>   Step firmly now. PHILOCTETES: As firmly as I can.

NEOPTOLEMUS:
>   The Greeks will rail at me. PHILOCTETES: Pay no attention.

NEOPTOLEMUS:
>   They may destroy my land. PHILOCTETES: I will be there.

NEOPTOLEMUS:
>   How can you help? PHILOCTETES: The bow of Heracles —

NEOPTOLEMUS:
>   The bow? PHILOCTETES: Will keep them off. NEOPTOLEMUS:
>   Then say farewell.

>   *Enter* HERACLES *above*

HERACLES:
>   Not yet, not yet. You shall not leave this place   1340
>   Until I speak. O son of Poias, hear.
>   This is the voice of Heracles. Your ear
>   Rings with the sound. You gaze upon his face.
>   From my abode on high I make my way
>   To show the destiny that Zeus decreed,
>   And stop your journey home. It was your need

That brought me here. Then harken, and obey.
But hear first the account of my own fortunes.
The arduous labors that I underwent
Won me the glorious immortality   1350
You now behold. Learn that you too are fated
To glorify your life through suffering.
You are to go with them, go back to Troy
To be delivered from your dread disease.
Then, chosen as the army's bravest man,
You are to slay the author of these evils,
Slay Paris with my bow. You are to sack
The city of Troy, to have the prize of valor
Given you by the Greeks, to carry home
To Oeta's heights the spoils of victory   1360
That will delight your father. Take a portion
With which to make an offering on my pyre
In memory of my bow. Son of Achilles,
What I have said I said to you as well.
Neither of you is strong enough alone
To conquer Troy. He needs your help, you his.
You are like lions that seek their prey together;
Each guards the other's life. To heal your wound
I will send down Asclepius to Troy
Since it is doomed to fall a second time   1370
Before my arrows. But remember this:
When you lay waste the land, reverence the gods,
For all things else are of less consequence
In the eyes of Zeus the father. Piety
Does not expire with men. It is immortal
Alike among the living and the dead.

PHILOCTETES:

O thou, whose voice I have so yearned to hear,
Whose face I see after so many days,
I will not disobey thee. NEOPTOLEMUS: Nor will I.

HERACLES:

Delay no more. The time is opportune   1380
To start your voyage, for the wind is fair.

Exit HERACLES

PHILOCTETES:

Let me now greet this land as I depart.
Farewell, O cave, companion of my vigils.
Nymphs of the streams and meadows, fare you well.
Farewell, O headland with your deep-voiced breakers,
Where in the inmost recess of my cavern
The wild wind drenched my head with flying spray,
And where Mount Hermes echoed to my outcry

When I was beaten by my storm of pain.
O springs, O Lycian fountain, now at last,   1390
At last I leave you, I who never hoped
For happiness like this. O sea-girt Lemnos,
I bid you now farewell. Be gracious to me.
Prosper my voyage to the destination
To which the counsel of my friends conducts me,
And mighty Fate, and that all-conquering god
By whose decree these acts have come to pass.

CHORUS:
      Come, all of us. But let us pray,
    Before we leave the land, that it may please
      The nymphs to send us forth upon our way   1400
        With favoring wind and seas.

42   After the death of Achilles his armor was to be awarded to the man who had rendered the next greatest service in the Trojan war. Odysseus won the award in preference to Ajax.

50   Agamemnon, king of Argos, the commander-in-chief, and his brother Menelaus, king of Sparta, whose wife, Helen, had been abducted by Paris, son of Priam, king of Troy. Agamemnon and Menelaus were the sons of Atreus, and are often referred to as the Atridae.

59   See line 50 note.

182   Instead of Odysseus, the Greek has "son of Sisyphus," a slurring reference to the legend that Odysseus' mother, Anticleia, was with child by Sisyphus when she married Laertes.

323   The name means "broad shield." See lines 554–5.

366   He was descended from Aeacus, the son of Zeus and Aegina. Aeacus had two sons: Telamon, father of Ajax, and Peleus, father of Achilles.

407   His name in Greek, Aias, was associated with the exclamation ai ai = "alas." The play on words here and in the case of Eurysaces (555–6) is untranslatable.

554–5   See line 323 note.

624   After Ajax and Hector had fought in single combat (*Iliad*, Bk. vii), they exchanged gifts and "parted again, reconciled in friendship," (not so much friendship as mutual respect).

788   Zeus was his ancestor (see line 366 note.) In the first episode Odysseus addresses Athena as "you," but he is not there praying as Ajax is here.

839–908   In this lyric passage the sections in corresponding meter are: 839–47 and 879–87; 857–60 and 897–900; 865–8 and 905–8.

905   "Persistent" translates the Homeric epithet "much-enduring" or "patient," here used ironically. Odysseus is patient in biding his time to strike.

910   After the award of the armor, while he was in seclusion.

161

979 In the *Iliad* the girdle has nothing to do with Hector's death. After he has been killed by Achilles, he is dragged behind a chariot with ox-hide thongs.

1009 Shameful because they would not have been killed in battle, as Ajax had not been. Ajax regarded his suicide as honorable. See lines 456–8.

1063 Before Helen's marriage to Menelaus the rivalry among her suitors was so great that Odysseus proposed that they should all swear to support the man Helen chose and to avenge any wrong that he might suffer as a result of his marriage.

1071–2 In comparison with an armored soldier (a hoplite) an archer was looked down upon, the implication being that he fought from a distance in order to escape hand-to-hand combat.

1131ff. Teucer wants to make sure that the body will not be disturbed until he finds a grave. With the boy touching it the body is under the protection of Zeus (in his capacity of guardian of suppliants), the gods of the underworld, and the shade of Ajax himself. The locks of hair symbolize the devotion of the individuals to the dead and are a substitute for primitive self-immolation.

1165 This is not the royal *we*. Agamemnon refers to himself and Menelaus.

1202 Teucer's mother was Hesione, daughter of King Laomedon of Troy. Apollo and Poseidon built the walls of Troy for Laomedon. When he refused them their promised reward, Poseidon sent a sea-dragon to ravage the country. Hesione was to be sacrificed to it, when Heracles arrived. Laomedon promised her to Heracles if he rescued her, but when he had done so, Laomedon again broke his word. Whereupon Heracles led an expedition, including Telamon, against Troy, killed Laomedon and all his sons except Priam, and gave Hesione to Telamon.

1224 The competitors for a prize, or the volunteers for a mission, threw their lots (usually a small stone or a fragment of pottery) into a helmet or urn, which was then shaken. The man whose lot was first shaken out was the winner. A coward would choose a lot, such as a lump of wet earth, which would not come out.

1232–8 Pelops (the son of Tantalus, son of Zeus) was the king of Phrygia, in Asia Minor. For Atreus, see note on line 11 in *Electra*. The wife of Atreus, and mother of Agamemnon, was Aerope, daughter of the king of Crete. When he discovered her making love to a slave, he sent her to the king of Euboea with instructions (which were of course disregarded) to drown her.

1251 His own body, and the bodies of Tecmessa and Eurysaces.

1293 Because he begins to see that he faces a conflict in his duty.

36　This was Eurystheus, king of Argos, whom, by a stratagem of
Hera, Zeus' wife, Heracles was compelled to serve, and for whom
he performed his Twelve Labors. These are over before the play
opens.

38　Iphitus was the son of Eurytus. See lines 243–63.

75　Eurytus. See lines 243–63.

98–9　An obscure passage here interpreted as referring to the Helles-
pont and the Pillars of Hercules at the straits of Gibraltar.

157　Dodona was the most ancient of Greek oracles, situated in north-
western Greece in Epirus. The rustling of the leaves of the sacred
oak constituted the oracle, as interpreted by the priests (later,
the priestesses). The origin of the name for the priestesses, the
Doves, is obscure.

231　Ever since Heracles had left her, fifteen months earlier.

248　The malice was intended to be deadly for Heracles but proved
deadly for Eurytus himself.

340　Eros is the god of love.

359　Lichas' first account was true in that Heracles was thrown out
of the palace by Eurytus, killed Iphitus in revenge, and was
punished by Zeus with slavery. It was, however, false in sup-
pressing Heracles' real reason for attacking Oechalia and killing
Eurytus. Presumably he asked for Iole as a concubine before he
was thrown out of the palace.

369　Since Lichas' conduct was hardly treacherous, the Chorus may
also be thinking of Heracles.

404　The Greek reads: "at whom you look as if you did not know
her," but Iole is not present.

577　Shamed by having the charm fail to work.

582　Ironic ambiguity: the "work of my hands" may mean either
"woven by me," or "anointed with poison by me."

594　Again ironic ambiguity: the secondary meaning is "clad in strange

164

clothes to do the gods strange service" by being the sacrifice himself.

602   Hermes was, among other things, the messenger of the gods and hence the patron of messengers and heralds.

634   Ares, the god of war, roused to madness, symbolizes the fury that drove Heracles to destroy Oechalia, an act that marked the beginning of his return home.

817   Sophocles personifies the blood with which the robe is smeared. It is a compound of the deadly venom of the Hydra, in which Heracles had dipped his arrows, and the blood of Nessus himself.

857   The first death is that of Heracles. The Chorus have been told that he may be already dead and have said themselves that he cannot survive.

861   The Chorus's repeated questions presumably are intended to indicate a state of shock.

993   The goddess Pallas Athena, daughter of Zeus, was the guardian and comforter of her half-brother.

1051–65   Heracles enumerates six of his many feats of superhuman strength. One (1055–7) was his fight with the Centaurs which arose while they were entertaining him. The others were five of his Twelve Labors (see line 36 note): 1) the killing of the Nemean lion; 2) the killing of the Lernean Hydra, a monster whose nine heads doubled in number as fast as they were cut off; 3) the killing of the Erymanthian boar; 4) the obtaining of the Apples of the Hesperides, guarded by a dragon and the daughters of the giant Atlas, who held up the sky on his shoulders. In the usual form of the myth Heracles induced Altas to get the apples for him while he substituted for Atlas in holding up the sky; 5) the bringing back of the triple-headed dog Cerberus, who guarded the entrance to Hades. His mother was Echidna, half-woman, half-serpent.

1130   The grove of the Selli was the sacred precinct of the temple at Dodona (see line 157 note).

1208   Hyllus expects some frenzied outburst from Heracles.

2 Agamemnon's brother, King Menelaus of Sparta, was the husband of Helen, the most beautiful woman in the world. The goddess of love, Aphrodite, in a beauty contest with Hera and Athena, bribed the judge to choose her by promising him Helen. When the judge, who was Paris, son of king Priam of Troy, subsequently ran off with Helen, the Greek leaders united to bring her back. The result was the Trojan War.

6 Inachus, a river god, was the legendary first king of Argos and the father of Io. Io, loved by Zeus, was changed into a cow by Hera, Zeus' wife. Driven by a gadfly, she wandered over the whole earth until Zeus induced Hera to restore her own form.

7 Lycius is a name for Apollo, the sun-god, in his aspect of protector of flocks and herds.

8 Hera (see line 6 note).

11 The sufferings of the house of Pelops illustrate the Greek belief in an inherited curse. The founder of the family was Tantalus, a son of Zeus and a favorite of the gods. Made insolent by his good fortune, he tried to test the gods' power of discrimination by offering them at a banquet the flesh of his own son, Pelops. Demeter, grieving for her lost daughter, inattentively ate a portion of Pelops' shoulder, but the other gods recognized the deception. They punished Tantalus by putting him in Hades up to his neck in water with boughs laden with fruit before his eyes, and by having the water and fruit constantly elude his efforts to drink or eat (hence: to tantalize). Pelops, restored to life by the gods and given an ivory shoulder, brought a further curse on his house. To win the hand of Hippodamia, daughter of Oenomaus, king of Pisa, Pelops had to risk his life in a chariot-race against the king, who had supernaturally swift horses. However he (or Hippodamia) bribed the king's charioteer, Myrtilus, to remove a pin fastening a wheel to its axle. Hence Pelops won. Later, however, he quarreled with Myrtilus and threw him into the sea, where he drowned cursing Pelops. Pelops lived happily (though his sister Niobe's life was tragic; see line 149 note), but the curse fell upon his descendants. His sons were Atreus and Thyestes. Thyestes seduced his brother's wife. In revenge Atreus killed Thyestes' two sons and served their flesh to Thyestes, who, lacking god-like wisdom, ate them. Following the instructions of an oracle he then committed incest with his daughter, Pelopis, in order to beget the son who would

avenge him; this son was Aegisthus. Atreus had two sons, Agamemnon and Menelaus (see line 2 note), who married two sisters, Clytemnestra and Helen. To placate Artemis, whom he had offended, Agamemnon sacrificed his daughter Iphigenia, so that the goddess would stop the adverse winds that were keeping the Greek army from sailing to Troy. To avenge this sacrifice Clytemnestra took Aegisthus as her lover, and, when Agamemnon returned from Troy, the pair brought about the king's death.

16 Pylades was the son of the king of Phocis to whom Orestes had been entrusted for safe-keeping as a child.

45 Phanoteus was a Phocian chieftain.

86–121 In the Greek the correspondence between the two stanzas is not exact.

108 The nightingale was Procne, the sister of Philomela and the wife of King Tereus. After seducing his sister-in-law, Tereus cut out her tongue to prevent her from informing his wife. But Philomela wove her story into a tapestry which she sent Procne. Procne then killed Itys, or Itylus, her son by Tereus, cooked him, and served him to his father. When Tereus discovered this, he pursued them to kill them, but the gods transformed all three: Procne into a nightingale, Philomela into a swallow, and Tereus into a hawk. The Latin poets, and following them the English poets, reverse the roles of the sisters, Philomela becoming the mother of Itys and a nightingale.

113 Electra invokes: 1) Hades and Persephone, the king and queen of the underworld, where Agamemnon now dwells; 2) Hermes, who brought him there in his capacity of psychopompos, or conductor of the dead. 3) the curse he called down upon his murderers, here thought of as a supernatural power that rouses the Furies to action; 4) the Furies, or Erinyes, themselves, the goddesses of vengeance.

144 The nightingale (see line 108 note) is Zeus' herald as the harbinger of spring.

149 Niobe (sister of Pelops; see line 11 note) was the wife of Amphion, regent of Thebes after the death of King Pentheus. During the ceremonies in honor of the goddess Leto and her children Apollo and Artemis, Niobe boasted of herself and her fourteen childen in comparison with the goddess and her two. In revenge Leto had all of Niobe's children killed and Niobe

herself transformed into a stone from which a stream of water continually flowed.

153   The Greek gives their names: Chrysothemis and Iphianassa.

182   The cry was the prophetic lament of Cassandra, daughter of King Priam of Troy, whom Agamemnon had brought back as his concubine and slave. She was killed with Agamemnon.

183   Agamemnon's own death shriek.

186   The offspring of lust and trickery was the act of murder.

250   Furies (see line 113 note).

299   The gifts were libations and other articles such as flowers or cakes.

419   Mangled by cutting off his hands and feet, originally to prevent his taking vengeance.

452   The spirit of Agamemnon was aiding the gods.

455   Furies (see line 113 note).

464   Pelops (see line 11 note).

466   Myrtilus (see line 11 note).

518   Artemis, the twin sister of Apollo, is the goddess of the moon and the hunt. All wild animals, especially deer, are sacred to her.

549   Electra regards Aegisthus as an enemy primarily because he aided in the murder of Agamemnon, but also because, as the son of Thyestes, he was the enemy of all the descendants of Atreus (see line 11 note).

599   The dream (391–7) might have been favorable in that the fruitful scepter now belonged to Aegisthus, or unfavorable in that it was Agamemnon who planted it.

608   Chrysothemis, Iphianassa, and her children by Aegisthus (543).

611   What remained was her wishes for her hostile children.

642   The prize was probably a wreath of laurel leaves.

663   The places were determined by the order in which the lots (fragments of pottery or small stones) were shaken from a helmet.

680   This was one of the two teams from Libya.

773   Apollo, the sun-god, should reveal the guilt with his rays, and Zeus should smite the sinner with his thunderbolts.

782-5   The Chorus try to console Electra by pointing to the example of Amphiaraus, husband of Eriphyle, the sister of the king of Argos. When Polyneices, son of King Oedipus, was driven from Thebes by his brother Eteocles, he came to Argos, among other places, to seek help in attacking Thebes. Amphiaraus refused because, as a prophet, he foresaw the outcome. Adrastus, the king of Argos, urged him to go. Finally the two agreed to leave the decision to Eriphyle. Having been bribed by Polyneices, she decided that he should go. As he left, he cursed her and called on his son Alcmaeon to avenge his death. The Thebans defeated the allies, and during the flight Amphiaraus was swallowed up when the earth was split by a thunderbolt. His wife was, therefore, responsible for his death and is spoken of as his murderess. Later he came to be worshiped as a god of the underworld. The Chorus wishes to suggest that Agamemnon, though he cannot be avenged, can still be honored.

786-7   Electra weeps because she is conscious of the difference between the two men. The Chorus suppose she is thinking of the likeness between them—each killed by his wife—and is about to say so, but Electra interrupts to point out that Amphiaraus was avengened by a champion. This was his son Alcmaeon, who killed his mother. The Chorus, admitting this fact, change the conclusion of their sentence. The translation is more specific than the original in order to make the allusion less obscure.

992   The illusion that the two sisters could ever agree.

1001   Themis is the goddess of divine justice.

1021   "Those who mourn" are the spirits of her unavenged father and her brother.

1196   A line of the original is here lost.

1257-8   Ostensibly she means the urn containing the ashes. In reality she means the retribution they are planning.

169

1276–7   Even what is morally ugly, for example, their pleasure in the news of Orestes' death. There is a similar ambiguous play on words in the Greek.

1330–1367   The authorities agree that this passage is made up of a strophe and an antistrophe, but they do not agree on whether or not the correspondence between them is exact. If it is, there must be gaps in the text since the antistrophe is shorter. Here, the correspondence is close, but not exact.

1374–1400   The speeches of Electra and Orestes are deliberately ambiguous.

5 Malis is in northern Greece on a deep gulf separating the island of Euboea from Thessaly. The chief mountain is Oeta, the site of Heracles' death. See lines 692–5.

75 All the suitors of Helen, Odysseus included, bound themselves by oath to come to her husband's aid if he was robbed of her.

79 The bow belonged originally to Apollo, who gave it to Heracles. As a reward for lighting his funeral pyre, Heracles gave it, together with the arrows dipped in the poisonous blood of Nessus the centaur, to Poias, the father of Philoctetes, or, as in this play, to Philoctetes himself (see lines 653, 764ff).

135 Hermes was, among other things, the herald and messenger of the gods, the god of commerce, and hence the god of cheating and theft.

189 For Chryse, see lines 252–9, 1252ff.

251 Odysseus, Agamemnon, and Menelaus. Cephallenia was an island near Ithaca and part of Odysseus' realm.

311 Menelaus was king of Sparta, Agamemnon king of Mycenae.

343 Sigeum was the promontory on which Troy stood.

362 Odysseus saved his body from being carried off by the Trojans.

372 See line 401.

379–86 The country of Troy was also called Phrygia. The Chorus invoke the chief divinity of the land, the great Earth Mother, the Phrygian Cybele, identified with Rhea, the mother of Zeus. Pactolus was the river on which Sardis was situated, a famous center of her worship. She is often represented as riding on a lion.

394 Ajax the elder (or the greater), son of Telemon, was Odysseus' rival for the armor of Achilles. On losing, he committed suicide. Ajax the younger (or the less) was the son of Oileus, king of the Locrians. It was this Ajax who was killed for defying the lightning of Zeus.

401 Sisyphus, king of Corinth, a great rascal, the cleverest of mankind, who could outwit Death himself (see lines 607–9 note).

Odysseus was bought because when Laertes paid the "bride-price" for his mother, she was already pregnant by Sisyphus.

405   King of Pylos, the wise counselor of the Greeks.

418   Patroclus was killed while wearing Achilles' armor. His death brought Achilles back into the fighting.

426   Homer describes him as railing at the leaders.

607-9   When about to die, Sisyphus told his wife simply to throw his body into the street. Hades was so shocked at the neglect of his funeral rites that he allowed him to return to earth long enough to punish her. Once back, he disobeyed and lived to old age.

653   See line 79 note.

661-4   In contrast to Philoctetes, who has just shown his gratitude to Neoptolemus, Ixion is the great example of ingratitude. Since there was no human means of purifying Ixion from the crime of murdering his father-in-law, Zeus himself did so, after carrying Ixion to Olympus. Thereupon Ixion attempted to make love to Hera. Sophocles omits the fact that the wheel to which he was bound was fiery.

690   The Chorus presumably do not know about the spring that Odysseus spoke of at the opening of the play.

693ff.   Seeing Philoctetes, the Chorus resume their role in support of Neoptolemus.

698-700   Heracles, here equipped like a Homeric warrior. The fire is that of the pyre on which he was burned, and possibly the lightning of Zeus, as a storm accompanied Heracles' apotheosis.

745   The gods might be jealous of any mortal fortunate enough to possess so sacred an object.

764   Apparently there was once a volcano on Lemnos (see lines 948-9 note).

805ff.   This vague stanza has been interpreted in various ways. Here "do it" (809) means to get possession of the bow and leave before Philoctetes wakes. What Neoptolemus means to do is to take Philoctetes with them, a plan that will certainly lead to trouble.

815   This contradicts what the Chorus have just said about light sleeping. They are, however, now hoping to persuade Neoptolemus that he can leave without disturbing Philoctetes.

948-9   Philoctetes invokes the local deities. When Hephaestus was hurled from Olympus by Zeus, he fell on Lemnos. The flame, a volcano, was explained as coming from his forge. Hephaestus was the god of fire, the smith, armorer, and builder of the gods. Odysseus invokes the higher authority of Zeus.

987-8   To avoid service Odysseus feigned madness by plowing with an ox yoked with an ass. Palamedes, the envoy of the Greeks, tricked him by laying his infant son in front of the plow. By stopping, Odysseus betrayed his sanity. In the *Odyssey* Homer had Odysseus go willingly.

991-2   Any difference of opinion between Agamemnon and Menelaus on the one hand and Odysseus on the other as to who was responsible for abandoning Philoctetes must have occurred before the play opens. In his first speech Odysseus tells Neoptolemus that he followed the generals' orders. In 251ff Philoctetes calls all three responsible.

1000-4   The Greeks would not have sought Philoctetes unless the war had been going badly for them, a state of affairs which shows the gods' concern for justice.

1230   Odysseus lied not merely in tricking Philoctetes but in twice threatening him in the name of the whole army.

1259   Asclepius was Apollo's son, the first physician, worshiped after his death as the god of medicine.

1295-6   The armor was made by the god Hephaestus. See line 948 note.

1359-61   Laomedon, king of Troy, broke his promise to give Heracles a reward for saving the life of his daughter Hesione. Accordingly Heracles captured Troy with the help of Telamon, father of Ajax; Peleus, father of Achilles; and others. Laomedon and all his family were slain except for his son, Priam, and Hesione, who became Telamon's wife.

173